# ROOMS YOU MAY HAVE MISSED

## UMBERTO RIVA

## BIJOY JAIN

Mirko Zardini

Canadian Centre for Architecture
Lars Müller Publishers

# ROOMS
# YOU MAY
# HAVE
# MISSED

# UMBERTO RIVA

9 In Milan, November 2013

9 **Via Vigevano**
10 **Everything is designed**
13 **Angles, colours, constraints**
16 **Landscapes and paths: the corridor, for example**
19 **Vertical landscapes: the stairs, for example**
21 **Ponti's eyes, Riva's ways of seeing**
22 **Close-ups: the details**
24 **Too large, too small: the motives of a closet**
25 **Against furniture: transformed tables**
26 **Never only one thing**
28 **Inhabitants**

30 Selected projects by Umberto Riva

32 Houses for temporary living
38 Casa Frea
54 Veronese
58 Casa Insinga
70 Casa Miggiano
84 Casa Righi

98 In Montreal, 28 February–5 March 2015
Giovanni Chiaramonte / Umberto Riva

119 May 2015

126 28 February–5 March 2015
Giovanni Chiaramonte / Bijoy Jain

# BIJOY JAIN

146 In Mumbai and Alibag, June 2014

146 **Mumbai–Alibag**
149 **Studio Mumbai as architectural practice**
152 **Wood, stones, bricks**
155 **Brooks, rain, basins, wells**
157 **The domestic landscape: the courtyards**
161 **Place, time, energy**
163 **Alibag–Mumbai**

168 Selected projects by Bijoy Jain

170 Weavers' Studio
184 House in Chennai
194 Saat Rasta
208 House in Ahmedabad
220 Copper House II

235 Biographies
238 Acknowledgements

Why do architecture is a question that is impossible
to answer without examining our most personal
convictions. Certainly the majority of responses
today would be very different than the ones we would
have been able to give twenty or thirty years ago,
before architecture—that 2 percent of the production
of buildings that is, more or less, recognized as such
how to define the remaining 98 percent would be
an interesting topic; is it a single, uniform mix?)—
began operating as an integral part of a more general
system of marketing, branding, and communication
that included both public and private buildings,
without distinction.

And certainly the majority of responses would have
been different in the 1920s and 1930s, and, at least
in Europe, during the postwar period, when a large part
of the Continent, armed with the new modern princi-
ples that had been established during the devastating
experience of World War II, began a rapid process of
reconstruction. It was a desolate period, but one that
was also full of hope for a better future, driven by
faith in an inevitable progress, in science and technology,
and confident in the role of disciplines such as architecture and urbanism.

Assuming that those interested in the question are
also capable of providing a convincing answer, we
can consider a second question: that is, how architecture can help us understand and, in part, transform
the different worlds in which we live.

## Via Vigevano

Umberto Riva and Bijoy Jain sit around a table in Riva's home studio on Via Vigevano in Milan. We're drinking tea and eating sweets that Emilio Scarano, Riva's assistant for the past few years, just bought from what we will soon discover is an excellent Neapolitan pastry shop—Emilio is of Neapolitan heritage—merely a few hundred metres away. It is one of the few "normal" stores (like butcher shops and hardware stores, for example) remaining of the kind that, until twenty or thirty years ago, characterized most of the streets around where we are, in the Ticinese and Porta Genova area of the city. Today these stores have become exceptions among the wine bars, cafés, gelato shops, and restaurants that have slowly transformed the streets of the area into a triumph of the happy hour—a rite that persists in Milan, where it has its own distinct expression. These new businesses represent the ideal extension of *Milano da bere*,[1] an attitude that characterized the city in the 1980s alongside the emergence of an apparent well-being and a diffuse hedonism. It's a Milan in which Riva is uneasy, a long way from the frugality and discretion that he once appreciated in a city that has now disappeared.

Riva has lived in this *casa di ringhiera* since 1982.[2] It is accessed by a cobblestone courtyard that contains a few plants and is

a slogan derived from an advertising campaign that suggests both drinking within the city and drinking or taking the city itself.

. *casa di ringhiera* is an apartment in a large complex with shared balconies with railings, or *ringhiere*, that give type its name.

Vigevano; the courtyard leading to Riva's studio
s from a video by Studio RGB/XYZ

now used as a parking lot serving the apartments and the few offices in the building (for example, the architectural firm that occupies part of the ground floor). Climbing the stairs to the first floor and crossing a walkway onto which other apartments face, you reach the entrance of Riva's studio. The other rooms in his apartment look out onto Via Vigevano.

Riva has always preferred to remain somewhat separate from the official world of architecture. This has been his refuge; he has lived and worked in the same small space for all of these years, cultivating a personal vision of the world and of the architect's work. From here he has observed, with disenchantment and melancholy, the disappearance of the Milan he once identified with, and has continued nevertheless to work in the same way.

## Everything is designed
After moving to Via Vigevano, Riva worked alone, though more recently he works with the help of a few assistants, a maximum of one or two young architects. It is here that he completed the renovation of Casa Frea.

Ezio Frea, the client, died a few years ago, and now the house is uninhabited. Frea was a photographer who started his practice taking photographs of tourists in Piazza Duomo in Milan (often posing with corn kernels in their hands, to attract the pigeons), and he hired Riva to convert a small townhouse into a family residence. The building was constructed in the 1920s for railroad workers. The house, with limited square footage and a small

arden in the back, consisted of two levels with a conventional
oor plan: entryway, living room, and kitchen on the ground floor,
vo rooms on the first floor, and an attic.

iva has never refused a job, big or small. This explains the
reat variety found in his work: a house, an apartment, a school,
lamp, a church, a table, a chair, a frame, shipyards. He has
ways lived modestly, reducing his requirements to a minimum.
or a time, Casa Frea is his only project, and he dedicates some
ears to it, designing each element of the house, every detail from
e fireplace to the mirrors, from the hinges of the doors to
e steps of the staircase. His work, which becomes a continuous
rocess of design, serves as a kind of personal therapy with
spect to the difficulties of everyday life. At the same time
constitutes an inevitable necessity in the face of the ongoing
volution of things and the constant incomprehensibility
problems. Riva's projects are explorations that could go on
definitely if some external event did not intervene to interrupt
em. They develop through rethinking and progressively
eeper study, by a sequence of approximations; the solution
always a temporary solution.

his continual work translates into technical drawings often
ccompanied by perspective sketches that overlap on the
me sheet, mixing different scales. On the one hand, they are
struments of exploration that simultaneously take into account
aterials and the perception of the inhabitant. But they are
so accurate descriptions and instructions for a group of trusted

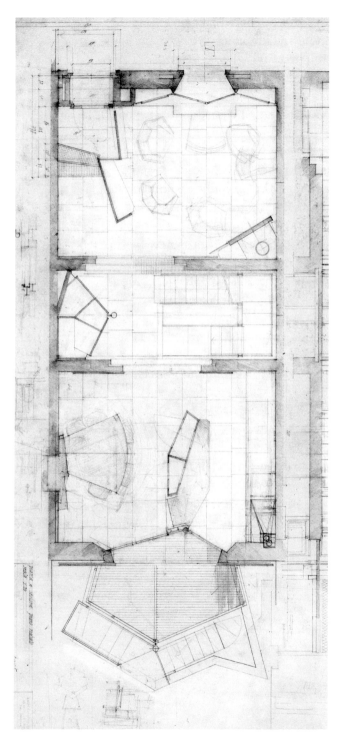

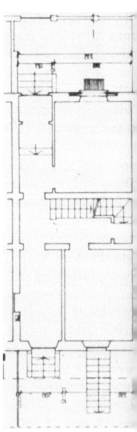

Details of drawings showing the renovated and original plans of the ground floor, Casa Frea

tisans who have accompanied him for decades: the carpenter
ontin, the blacksmith Bagatti. They are black and white pencil
awings, traced with a parallel rule, triangles, and compasses,
on the mechanical drafting table that still occupies part of the
udio. Although in recent years the computer has become part
his office, it represents merely a means of transcription carried
t by Emilio.

## ngles, colours, constraints

ily in recent years has Riva reduced his practice of painting.
r many years, it was his principal occupation during his stays
Lago Maggiore, in Ghiffa.

va's paintings are in mixed media with pencil or pastel, explor-
ions of geometry and colour that resurface in his architectural
awings and realized work. Unlike his plans for installations,
ildings, or apartments such as Casa Insinga and Casa Frea, where
terrupted diagonal lines construct a dynamic system of paths,
rpetually directing and redirecting movement, the paintings
e closed systems; energy accumulates inside them, confined
ithin the physical limits of the canvas. *Everything within the
iges* is the title of a painting from 1984. In *Piccolo aquilone
mall Kite)*, from 1985, an eight-sided figure is fractured into
er-smaller and narrower triangles, their outlines sharpened
the juxtaposition of high-contrast colours—ruddy red-brown,
ral, emerald green, golden yellow.

The irregular, angular schemes developed in his paintings allow
Riva to define and redefine the spaces of apartments and houses
by turning banal constraints into meaningful parts of a larger
whole. Existing walls (for example, in Casa Insinga) and surrounding structures (as in Casa Miggiano) become sounding boards. In
one of his first jobs in Stintino, in Sardinia, these angles demarcate
the terracing that regulates the passage from street level to the
buildings, which are sunk into the soil for protection from the
strong wind that whips the coast. The colours also highlight
contrasts, as with the red plaques placed at points of convergence
between Riva's constructed walls and the existing galleries
in his most recent exhibition installation, at the CCA, or become
a means to break the geometry, such as in the courtyards of
the houses in Sardinia. Other times, as in Casa Righi, they flag
the presence of the new and the old.

Casa Righi, located on the southern periphery of Milan in what
was an area of factories and public housing, spreads over two
floors of a repurposed building in a complex of warehouses. From
the ground floor, which houses a psychiatrist's office and a small
bedroom, you take a metallic staircase to a new mezzanine, where
there is a second bedroom, and to the top floor, where you find the
kitchen, living room, and terrace. Riva maintains the height of
the previous industrial space at the entrance and in the bedroom
on the ground floor. The insertion of the mezzanine and the open
staircase produces a sequence of spatial compressions and expan-
sions and allows for the creation of galleries and small interior
windows, as well as vertical cuts that yield diagonal views. When

*Piccolo aquilone*, 1985; courtyard, Casa Tabanelli
Painting and photograph by Umberto Riva

e reach the top floor we find the double-height space again,
 its original dimensions, articulated by the volume of a storage
oset that constricts the area near the entrance. To the right,
 wall and shallow table screen the kitchen and a bigger table
 hind. The presence of these new elements is emphasized by
 e use of colour: dusty red, intense green, and the paler colours
 the kitchen—the soft yellow of the tabletop, the rose pinks of
 e cabinets. To accentuate the contrast, all the walls are kept a
 utral industrial grey that absorbs the presence of the existing
 lumns, while on the ceiling, blocks of grey alternate with
 ghter surfaces, marking the presence of the concrete beams of
 e old building. The existing industrial structure welcomes
 va's intervention with both grace and indifference. The additions
 pear fragile, an installation that, like the act of dwelling, is
 ways temporary, ready to disappear, to be substituted by other
 alls, other furniture, other inhabitants.

 any architects consider their projects struggles against
 e limitations imposed by the location, the existing building on
 hich they're called to intervene, the materials, the budget,
  the client's wishes. For Riva the opposite is true: projects are
 rn and grow around their limits in small, deliberate moves.
 ch constraint becomes an opportunity to enrich the project,
 epening it, incorporating a new aspect of reality.

cal openings, Casa Righi
tographs by Santi Caleca

## Landscapes and paths: the corridor, for example

I first visited Casa Insinga at the end of the 1980s, shortly before it was inhabited. Today, it is a late morning in April, and Mr. Insinga, an engineer, is again not home. The woman who takes care of the apartment for a few hours each week welcomes us in. While we move through the rooms, she continues to iron in the kitchen, near a window. The building, located on Via Arena in Milan, not far from Riva's home studio, was bombed during the war and has been almost completely rebuilt. Only the external facade remains of the original structure. The apartment consists of two wings, requiring a long corridor to connect the entrance to the living space at the apartment's centre, where the views and light are most favourable. The new walls break the rule of the right angle and avoid any correspondence with the position of the perimeter walls. As in many other projects—Casa Frea, for example—our gaze can wander along unexpected diagonals in a landscape marked by pathways rather than a typical organization of isolated rooms.

In Casa Insinga, Riva transforms the traditional corridor, which would link the entryway to the living room, into an irregular path that contracts and expands. The wall on our left as we enter folds and juts with slight inclines and fissures. It is no longer a linear and uniform element but a succession of episodes: the metal coat rack; the circular staircase leading to the terrace, with its threshold covered in terrazzo flooring; the glass brick that brings light to a half bath; and finally a wood panel with a large internal window, partly clear glass and partly opaque,

Moving from entry to living room, Casa Insinga
Photographs by Giovanni Chiaramonte

hich assures that the kitchen table receives daylight from
oth the courtyard and the street. This panel, which resembles
store window, bends to form the doorway that divides the
tchen dining area and the living room. On the other side of
e hallway, to the right, the recessed windows overlooking the
ourtyard—highlighted by protruding, blue-grey moulding—
e also detached from the wall plane, further articulating the
ith toward the living room.

these few metres Riva offers us an example of how he dis-
antles and reformulates space: instead of presenting us with the
iiform and regular space of a corridor, he orchestrates a new
rrative, rich with surprises. His work is a declared struggle
ainst the poverty of the spaces—and therefore the experiences,
d the banal dullness of the elements (corridors, doors, windows,
ilings, and floors)—that we usually find in our dwellings. It
an attempt to dig deeper, to give the complexity of things, of the
orld, back to us. This feeling is behind his admiration for
rlo Scarpa, for his incessant research, dictated by the desire to
t take anything for granted but to call into question each and
ery element of the plan and the construction.

new surprise awaits us in the living room: the fireplace, incor-
rated into a slightly curved green and red partition, dominates
e room, defining on one side the way to the bedrooms and
the other a seating area that invites conversation. Upon enter-
g the living space we see a table placed against the wall, sloping
ght as though to prompt us to veer that way, deviating from

es on living room ceiling, Casa Insinga
ograph by Francesco Radino

the straight line of the path. If we turn around we discover a completely different view of the progression we just completed, and on the right, when the folding door is open, we see through to the end of the kitchen, where we can make out the figure of a person ironing dress shirts with great expertise.

If we look down at the point of transition between our arrival path and the living room, we note how a change in the pattern of the floor treatment reinforces this change in geometries. Looking farther in, toward the bedrooms, we understand how the path extends to penetrate the larger living space, concluding with a metal strip wide enough to be perceived as a threshold. If, instead, we raise our eyes, we notice how the ceiling is marked with ridges—small dimples that are barely visible in the unvarying, grey light of the morning but will project shadows later on in the day, when the sun cuts through the room, bringing to life otherwise dull and insignificant surfaces. (These dimples will reappear in a different form in the house in Otranto, in the kitchen and living room, as a triangular cut into the ceiling section that regulates the presence of light in the various spaces.)

At the end of Casa Insinga's living room, an oak wall concludes the itinerary. It incorporates shelves of different depths that hold paintings or books, along with cabinets and a door. In the far corner a panel of blue glass shines. Only now do we remember having seen it at the entrance, on the back of the door as we closed it. The path is completed. Beyond the wall lies the private space of the bedrooms, the bathrooms, and a walk-in closet.

# ertical landscapes: the stairs, for example

ı Casa Frea, Riva also transforms the traditional typology of the ownhouse into a new domestic landscape. In this case, however, e found himself having to overcome the constraint of the load-earing brick walls that defined the organization of the existing ouse. To work around this difficulty, Riva widened the openings round the staircase in the house's core, inserting glazed transom indows over the metal I-beams that now span each door frame. ı this way it is possible for light to spread throughout the house, ıd for our gaze to penetrate from one side of the residence to ıe other. From the entrance we can already glimpse the dining rea and even the garden, through the filter of the veranda that rovides access to it.

ıt our wandering gaze isn't confined to only horizontal move-ents. The original staircase at the house's centre is substituted ith a metal one that gradually tightens as it rises. The roof ecomes a double skylight that controls light and the circulation ˙ air; on the top floor, the load-bearing walls are carved into to ˙eate niches. The stairway, once the darkest part of the house, is well of light, a new and surprising vertical landscape.

ıars later we discover another vertical tableau in Otranto, the space surrounding Casa Miggiano's stairwell. The house a new construction marked by the presence of an outdoor ˙ace wedged into its volume. This time the light in the stairway not diffuse, but cast down in concentrated shards. The aircase, with its slashes of light, balconies, and lateral views,

ɔ-bearing wall on ground floor and skylight at top of stairs, Casa Frea
tographs by G. Chiaramonte

becomes a vertical pathway punctuated with contrasts of light and shadow.

Casa Miggiano is not far from the old centre of Otranto. From there, a twenty-minute walk along the sea gives us the chance to observe the historic city that developed around the cathedral and the castle that dominates the city from above. By car, it's just a few minutes. We reach a familiar landscape—the new Italian suburbs. Our eyes, though accustomed to all that, grieve in a Gaddaesque way once again at the sight of large houses, town-houses, luxury apartment buildings, and condominiums.[3] The only reminders of the countryside are a few names, like that of Via dei Gelsi Mori, where we arrive. It is a name that evokes plants and fruit (*morus nigra*, or blackberries), all traces of which are gone, and that is now a common moniker for hotels and bed and breakfasts. From the street, the house appears as a wall notched with narrow windows or, more precisely, by a series of vertical cuts. The main attraction is, instead, the presence of a garden, a rarity in this proliferation of buildings, which continues until the boardwalk and flanks the remains of a neigh-bouring construction made of tuff.

At the far end of the garden, the house closes in on itself, articulated around an irregular, cut-out, triangular space at its centre; its curved wall seems to be the product of an

3  Carlo Emilio Gadda was a twentieth-century Milanese novelist, journalist, and intellectual well known for his observations and critiques of the Italian urban periphery after Fascism. Novels such as *L'Adalgisa* (1944), *Quer pasticciaccio brutto de via* (1957), and *La cognizione del dolore* (1963), among other writings, exemplify his way of looking at these conditions, which he described in *L'Adalgisa* using the Latin term *villula*.

West facade and view looking up along central staircase, Casa Miggiano
Photographs by Roberto Collovà (left) and U. Riva (right)

xternal force that, struggling, has slipped into and cleaved
1e compact volume, dividing it, but only partially, into two
uildings. A pergola indicates the path to the garden, a trace of
1is force that has marked the building. The internal staircase,
laced in correspondence with the courtyard, seems to be
1e only element that has withstood this force, though it has
een left deformed. The entire central space of the house
1us becomes its crux, and as we slowly ascend or descend
1e stairs we discover the startling results of this clash.

## onti's eyes, Riva's ways of seeing

1 the plans for Villa Planchart, built in Caracas in the 1950s,
iò Ponti draws in human figures and eyes and traces from
1em different possible sightlines turned toward the other rooms
r toward the garden and the surrounding landscape. Riva
 not so explicit in his designs, in which neither eyes nor figures
ppear. Nevertheless, it is not difficult to intuit their presence,
ot only in each plan but also in each section. The views he
onceives are wavering, pulled gradually in unexpected directions
; we move: horizontally, vertically, but also diagonally in
)ace, as in Casa Righi in Milan. From the bedroom on the mezza-
ne, it is in fact possible to look down into the room beneath
1d, by manipulating the opening of a narrow window, onto
le staircase.

nlike Ponti's sightlines, which are of equal length, Riva's
ver various distances, crossing the entire building or pausing on
mething nearby. Sometimes they point to grains of wood, or

room on mezzanine, Casa Righi
tograph by S. Caleca

BERTO RIVA

a particular aspect of a detail, or an unusual combination of materials. These oblique sightlines are ready to capture dissonances, divisions, and gaps that bring us into the complexity of the project, and of things. The traditional hierarchy of views no longer exists. Each element, even the apparently unimportant one, is equally relevant in the construction of the project, in the defining of spaces and internal scenes, in the creation of new narratives.

## Close-ups: the details

On a shelf in the studio on Via Vigevano, next to the large work-table, sits a group of lamps designed by Riva. Among these are two Veronese lamps, often turned on, one in carmine-coloured glass and the other in green. (The only colour that is still produced today is amber.) These "vases" in blown Murano glass rest on metal bases with the help of wedged wooden supports.

A characteristic trait of Riva's work is the juxtaposition of different materials, in which value distinctions disappear. What is interesting instead is the effect created by the contrast, by the unexpected combination of materials and attention. Generally the materials used are common: industrial Eternit panels for the house in Osmate, local stones in Stintino, floors made of industrial wood. The side table in the kitchen in Casa Insinga, a surface that also acts as a radiator cover, is a simple paving stone supported by a metal tube. These materials are made precious by the brilliant yellow and the detailing of the stand, not through their inherent qualities.

Detail of side table in kitchen, Casa Insinga; interior cable system, Veronese lamp
Photographs by G. Chiaramonte (left) and CCA (right)

 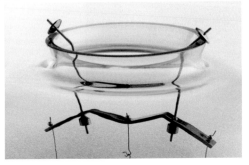

iva's details often turn out to be rich and articulated; we find
1 them the same complexity that distinguishes the architectural
roject as a whole. The small scale does not imply a process of
rogressively simplifying problems. On the contrary, his attention
) each component offers a new arena of study, as well as a chance
) explore new possibilities, once again without taking anything
)r granted. Their reduced physical scope makes Riva's approach
1d the intensity of his research, which consolidates on a few
oints, all the more evident. In this way, the details reproduce the
ame condition we find in his paintings, in which the limited
1rface of the paper accentuates their intensity.

7hile the metal cables of the Veronese, for example, support
 glass fragment that acts as a diffuser for the lamp's light,
1ey also become a real spatial structure that occupies and gives
1ape to the internal volume of the lamp. Riva invented this
rstem of cables and clamps in order to avoid piercing the glass.
his solution is dictated by a respect for materials, by an artisanal
.orality, which links Riva's work with that of Franco Albini.
n a list of architects he admires that Riva once prepared for
conference, Scarpa and Albini appear together.) This same
orality with respect to materials obliges Riva to avoid cutting
e Eternit panels in the house in Osmate. There, the large open-
gs are concentrated at the extremities, where they take the
rm of a loggia and a veranda, while the lateral openings are
duced to small, square windows placed at the seams between
vo panels.

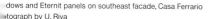
dows and Eternit panels on southeast facade, Casa Ferrario
tograph by U. Riva

## Too large, too small: the motives of a closet

Moving around in Riva's houses is always pleasant. The surprises that enrich our experience of the spaces are not merely dictated by the succession of individual scenes; very often they come from a sudden jump in scale, which is not only the result of details that catch our eye but also by the appearance of elements that are out of scale themselves, too large or too small with respect to the space in which they are situated.

Descending the stairs in Casa Frea, for example, we abruptly come to two tall, narrow walls made of wood. They are the doors of the closet that faces the stairs, placed at an unusual angle and occupying all of the available height. They appear to us even larger because we are squeezed into a reduced space. If we walk back up to the first floor, we find a small study that benefits from the presence of two windows. As we get closer, we feel dis-oriented; the windows seem to extend upward indefinitely. In fact, mirrors situated above them lengthen their presence beyond the limits of the ceiling, in a sort of artificial Baroque.

In Otranto, light and views of the sea are regulated through the contrast between very small window openings and the generous dimensions of the loggias and terraces on the upper floors. The for-mer control the sunlight that characterizes Apulia by selectively intensifying its effect. The first floor loggias, on the other hand, reclaim the size of Apulia's traditional porticoes, framing the nearby sea and historic centre of Otranto. Out on the terrace our view suddenly widens.

Openings onto terraces, Casa Miggiano; closet and mirrored panel, Casa Frea
Photographs by G. Chiaramonte

## Against furniture: transformed tables

When we enter Casa Insinga's living room, a table leaning against the wall gently guides us toward the centre of the space. The table can accommodate more guests by means of a mechanism visible through a glass porthole at its centre. But when the guests leave and we shorten the table again, the extra leaf does not disappear inside the structure, as is often the case, but instead folds back up along the wall. It does not exactly seem like a table, even if its use is never doubted, but rather the extension of a counter, a shelf, or a wooden wall; it belongs to this part of the room. The table on the first floor of Casa Frea is also reduced to a similarly anchored plane. One of its sides is supported by a leg—or, better yet, a wood panel. But on the other side, we discover that it is held up by a linchpin hooked into the windowsill from which it is suspended, and of which it is a continuation.

It would be easy to echo the idea that Riva designs furniture. On the contrary, his work on interiors aims to get rid of the traditional idea of furniture, of the mobility of tables and chairs, and instead to transform furniture into fixed elements that play a similar role as the walls, ceilings, floors, doors, windows, and fireplaces with which they compete to define architectural space. Closets and fireplaces are also walls, windowsills are long ledges, and tables are shelves hooked to the walls. His armchairs, the dimensions of which are exaggerated by their broad armrests, appear difficult to move, and not only because of their size or their weight. They can't

Windowsill and table in first-floor office, Casa Frea
Photograph by G. Chiaramonte

be moved because their position is dictated by the intersection of invisible threads that make up the fabric of the project— which again recall the knotted triangulations that appear in Riva's paintings.

## Never only one thing

For Riva, modernity is not able to offer us solutions, models, or new grounding for our work. Modernity is a state of affairs that must be continually explored, reviewed, called into question. Let us take as examples a few elements: doors, windows, floors, ceilings, stairs, and corridors. At the Venice Architecture Biennale, Rem Koolhaas tried to use these elements to define the new foundations of architecture, creating an exhibition of their evolution and of the solutions that decades of projects have produced. For Riva, on the other hand, modern tradition cannot provide prototypes, nor an ideal catalogue of answers to problems. Doors, windows, stairs, corridors, floors, and fireplaces are elements that should be questioned and reinvented over and over, not only by considering their technical features or their functions but also by recasting them as formal devices.

When we enter Casa Frea we discover that the windows are no longer only windows. First of all, they turn out to be folded, bent inward so as to enrich the banal external facade with a play of shadows. On the inside we find the same angled windows again, convex this time, almost reminiscent of bay windows turned inside out, which give a different

Windowsill in living room and exterior view of office window, Casa Frea
Photographs by G. Chiaramonte (left) and U. Riva (right)

patiality to the rooms—accentuating the concept of the
window as a mechanism for capturing external light, but also
drawing our eye and, at the same time, preventing us from
looking directly out, imposing on us to look diagonally. In the
living room Riva erases the presence of the wall toward the
street, substituting it with a system of display shelving of which
the window becomes a part, supported by a windowsill-shelf
and a series of cabinets that cover the radiators. The wall is dug
out to house the display shelving that angles in and converges
toward the (asymmetric) window, emphasizing its presence
in the room, off the flat plane of the wall. The lamp positioned
high on the wall to the right becomes a light box, filtering light
through blue and yellow glass that, at dusk, endows the
twilight with new hues.

By redeeming those elements generally considered to be merely
functional or auxiliary from their lack of significance, Riva
transforms them into real environmental sculptures. Each element
can be an object of exploration; each element has the potential
to become something else, to enter into a complex and dense
system of meaning and contribute to the overall narrative of
the house.

Even the drainpipe of the house in the forest in Osmate is no
longer a drainpipe, but becomes a structural element, an inclined
pillar (hollow, of course) that supports the canopy at the
entrance and defines its form. Another drainpipe, this time at
Casa Frea, is the load-bearing element and the fulcrum of the

Drainpipe holding up extended roof, Casa Ferrario; veranda in rear garden, Casa Frea
Photographs by U. Riva

composition of the veranda, a compressed hexagon that mediates the passage between the kitchen-dining room and the garden in the back. In his first jobs, on the houses in Stintino, Riva had already begun this process of deconstructing and altering architectural elements. In the second group of houses he built there, the roofs are no longer covered with the traditional tiling but with tiles made of red terracotta and blue ceramic. Today, they seem like awnings suspended above the brick walls, such that the buildings almost disappear. They are temporary tents absorbed by the soil on one side and vanishing into the sky on the other.

## Inhabitants

Conversations with Riva are full of pauses, silences, and ironic looks. They reveal an innate reluctance to talk about his own work, and to explain its motives. Nevertheless, he eventually supplies a polite response, or at least some clues, even if they may not be what we are expecting. He might confess that yes, it is true that he thought about how we could have perceived a certain space, about that light, about those colours. But then he begins to talk about our habits, about the practices and gestures that make up our daily lives. How we open that drawer, how we close that window. Where we place that object, or the pot, plates, and dish soap. And what do we do about the broom? And the clothes? And upon entering the house— where do we put our hat?

West facade, Case Di Palma
Photograph by U. Riva

uring the Milanese winter, Riva wears a black Borsalino
at. There is always a shelf for hats at the entrance to
s houses: a simple surface, but one that takes care of us
its small way. Noticing these considered moments,
e imagine him ever present, leaning on a wall or sitting
earby, observing us in order to understand the distance
etween his architecture and our lives.

at and hat racks, Casa Insinga and Casa Righi
otographs by G. Chiaramonte (left) and S. Caleca (right)

**HOUSES FOR TEMPORARY LIVING**

32   CASE DI PALMA
     Stintino, Sardinia
     1971–1972

36   CASA TABANELLI
     Stintino, Sardinia
     1974

37   CASA FERRARIO
     Osmate, Lombardy
     1975–1976

38   **CASA FREA**
     Milan, Lombardy
     Design: 1980–1982
     Construction: 1983–1984
     Furniture: Contin (Thiene, Veneto)

54   **VERONESE**
     1985
     Production: Barovier&Toso (Venice, Veneto)

58   **CASA INSINGA**
     Milan, Lombardy
     1987
     Furniture: Contin (Thiene, Veneto)
     Ironwork: Patelli (Bergamo, Lombardy)

70   **CASA MIGGIANO**
     Otranto, Apulia
     Design: 1989–1990
     Construction: 1991–1996

84   **CASA RIGHI**
     Milan, Lombardy
     2002–2003
     Furniture: Lino Contin (Thiene, Veneto)
     Metalwork: Maurizio Patelli (Brescia, Lombardy)

## CASE DI PALMA

The second commission for the family of a Milanese stockbroker, Case Di Palma is a collection of small cottages laid out within a long, thin building on a rocky Sardinian peninsula. The structure is seemingly embedded into the jagged landscape, a formal reference to the tuna-processing factories in the area. The complex contains three two-bedroom residences separated from one another by open-air courtyards and lined on their east and west facades by continuous porticoes. Oblique openings cut into these heavy stone walls frame views of the sea. Light also reaches the interiors from above, through coloured glass supported by the cement-pumice walls and between the checkered tiles on the roof.

## CASA TABANELLI

Casa Tabanelli is a group of linear buildings on the same peninsula designed for a contractor from Milan who knew the Di Palma family. Living areas for a single vacation house are dispersed across the two structures, which are constructed in brick and reinforced concrete and surfaced with the same local stone that appears in Riva's earlier projects in the area.

## CASA FERRARIO

Designed for a Milanese professional and his family of four who knew Riva through mutual friends, Casa Ferrario is a weekend vacation home in the woods near Lago Maggiore, sixty kilometres northwest of Milan. The house takes the form of a closed-off hexagonal shape set among dense oak, chestnut, pine, and birch trees. Its exteriors and roof are clad in Eternit, a low-cost corrugated fibre cement typically used in industrial construction. Natural light reaches the double-height living spaces on the main floor through a fibreglass skylight running along the spine of the roof, as well as through glass windows and doors cut out of the angled surfaces on the home's shorter edges. To the northeast, the plan dents inward to create space for a covered patio just outside the living and dining room; another smaller landing accompanies the bedrooms to the southwest.

## ASA FREA

ommissioned by a still-life photographer, Casa Frea the total renovation of an existing rowhouse in Milan. e structure is part of a neighbourhood built in the rly twentieth century to house state railway employees.

va's design carves new space from what was eviously a very divided plan. Widened doorways and ass panels inserted into load-bearing walls on either de of a central staircase allow transversal views ross the raised ground floor. The white-painted metal aircase acts as a vertical corridor; a skylight above sts patterned shadows down the stairway through the me's four stories. The rooms around this core are -articulated through the careful placement of designed ements, including partitions, a fireplace, a complex gular window system, and furniture constructed by e carpentry firm Contin.

h the entry level, a living room looks onto a small rden and Via Sant'Eusebio, while the kitchen and ning area behind the stairs lead to a veranda and ger garden. Upstairs, the first floor contains a bedroom, fice, and bathroom for the parents. Bedrooms and oath for two children are located on the second floor.

## ASA INSINGA

asa Insinga is a renovated corner apartment in Milan signed for a single occupant, a civil engineer who was professional contact of Riva's. Located in a central ighbourhood near Porta Ticinese, not far from Riva's dio, the apartment looks onto a courtyard behind and to Via Arena and a public green space in front.

e new plan shapes a progression toward a large ng room, the apartment's centre of gravity. At e entrance, a metal coat and hat rack is wedged tween the door and a curved wall, which encloses piral staircase leading to a terrace on the roof. k partitions set at slightly different angles, some-es lined with shelves, delineate a path passing the kitchen and other services on the left. To the ht, an angular, extendable locust-wood table aches to the wall; this table and a dark bent-metal stom fireplace organize the living area. Ridges on e plaster ceiling and glass panels above doorways ll light further inside the apartment, including ward bedrooms in the back.

## CASA MIGGIANO

Casa Miggiano is a four-story house in Otranto, a harbour city with Roman origins on the Adriatic coast. It was designed for a former mayor of Otranto and multiple generations of his family.

The house turns away from its neighbours—new con-structions in a conventional housing development—and instead orients itself south toward a garden and the sea beyond. A wedge-shaped void in the south facade lets in additional light and air and articulates the volume into two vertical elements, whose forms recall the farmhouses in the region. One half of the ground floor contains a separate apartment for the client's parents. A staircase in the centre links a larger kitchen and dining area on the ground floor with bedrooms, a study, and terraces above.

The house's reinforced concrete walls are covered in a tufa-lime stucco mixture and Lecce stone, common materials in this part of Apulia. The stucco mixture was allowed to oxidize in different ways to create a range of shades, from off-white to yellow, that further engages the light and shadows in the house's interior spaces.

## CASA RIGHI

Casa Righi is a home and psychiatrist's office on the industrial periphery of Milan designed for a friend of Riva's. The project converts the interiors of existing industrial workshops, traces of which are visible in the unpainted cement beams on the top level.

The ground floor contains the studio and a public waiting area with street entry, as well as a small bedroom only accessible through a door leading to a private staircase. A mezzanine inserted above the ground floor claims new space from the double-height building section. Cuts into the walls of a larger, triangular bedroom on this level create visual connections with the foyer on one side and the bedroom below on the other.

The first floor retains the full height of the original structure and includes the house's main living spaces. A dusty red partition visually separates the staircase from the living room, where floor-to-ceiling windows to the left and right provide views onto surrounding terraces. The far wall contains a large built-in bookcase. A custom cupboard sets off the kitchen; just behind, an adjacent laminated dining table is lit by a hanging Veronese lamp.

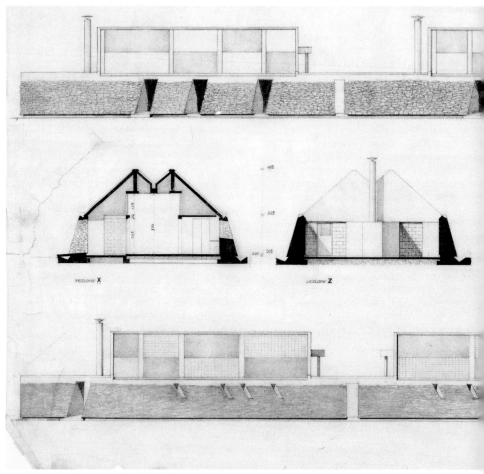

sezione X    sezione Z

Case Di Palma: Elevations and sections, 1:50, c. 1970
Graphite and transfer lettering on translucent paper, 54.9 × 125.8 cm. ARCH271193
All photographs of drawings by CCA

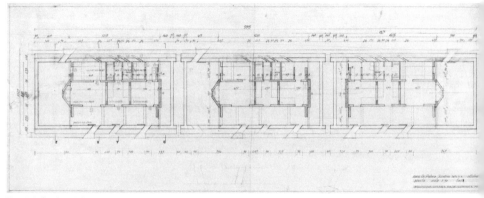

Plan, 1:50, October 1970
Graphite and transfer lettering on translucent paper, 50.4 × 131.9 cm. ARCH271139

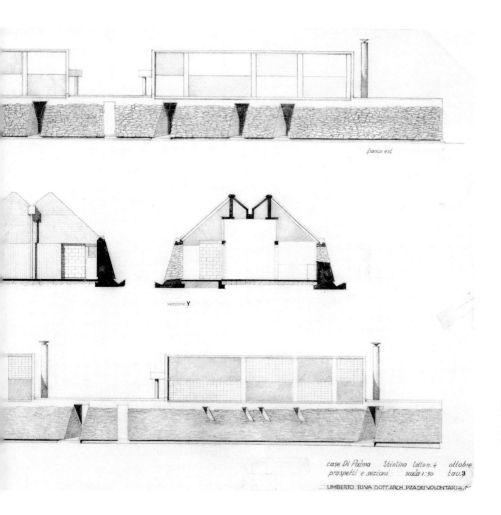

fianco est

sezione Y

case Di Palma    Stintino  lotton.4    ottobre
prospetti e sezioni       scala 1:50       tav.3
UMBERTO RIVA DOTT.ARCH. PZA DEI VOLONTARI 4,M

Case Di Palma: East facade, portico, and interior wall with coloured glass panels, c. 1972
Unless otherwise indicated, all photographs until page 95 by Umberto Riva

Casa Tabanelli: Courtyard on east facade, c. 1974

a Ferrario: Northeast facade, c. 1976

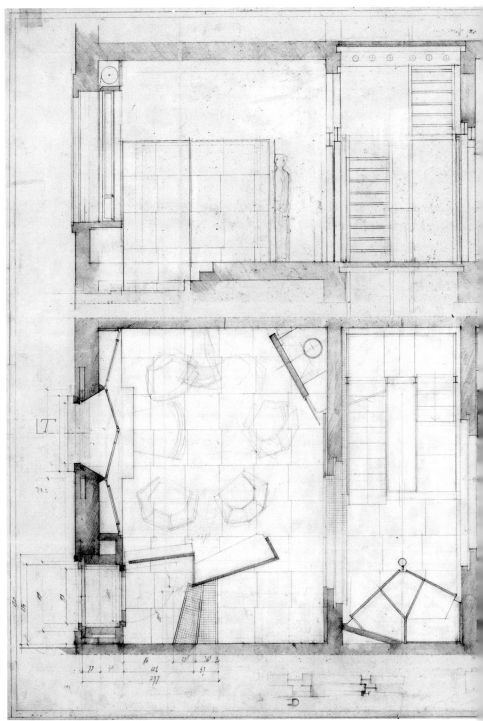

Plan and section of ground floor, 1:20, c. 1982
Graphite on drafting film with ink stamp and traces of transfer lettering, 60 × 87.8 cm. ARCH271180

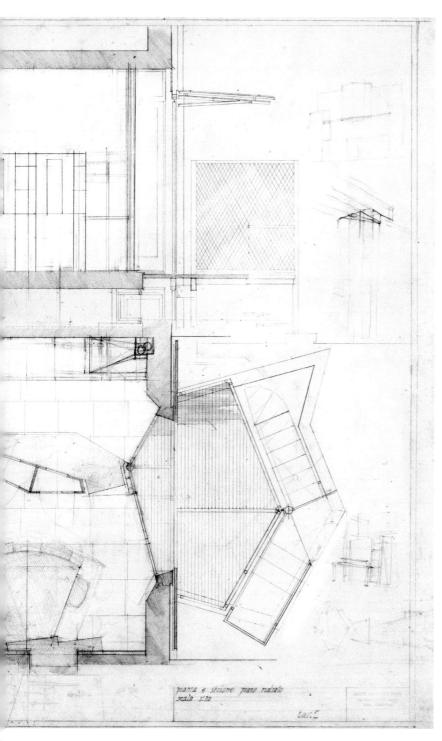

pianta e sezione piano rialzato
scala 1:20

tav. 5

Window system in living room, c. 1984
Photograph by Ezio Frea

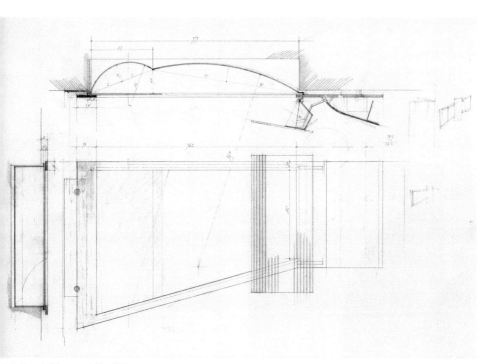

tail of lamp in living room, 1:10, c. 1982
aphite on translucent paper, 60 × 97.5 cm. ARCH271160

Spaces on ground floor from living room to kitchen, c. 1984
Photographs on top right and bottom left by E. Frea

> Elevation, plan, and perspective sketch of living room, 1:10, c. 198
Graphite on translucent paper, 96.8 × 60 cm. ARCH271190

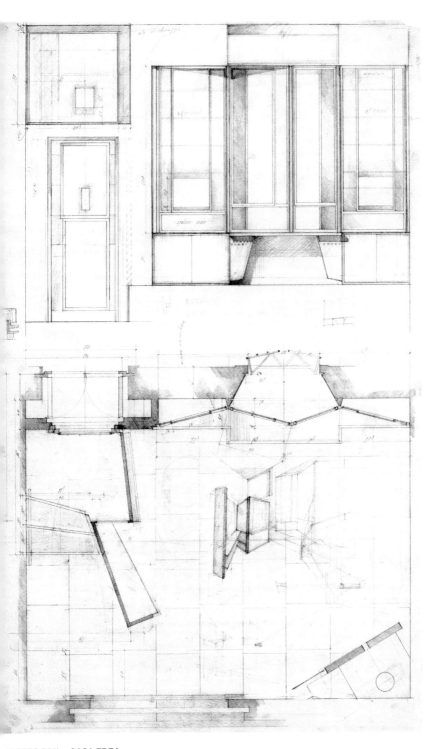

View of stairwell and kitchen from living room, c. 1984

> View from kitchen to veranda in rear garden, c. 1984

Closet at base of stairs, c. 1984
Gelatin silver print, 30.64 × 23.5 cm. Photograph by G. Chiaramonte

> Detail of closet, 1:1, c. 1982
Graphite on translucent paper, 62.5 × 90 cm. ARCH271169

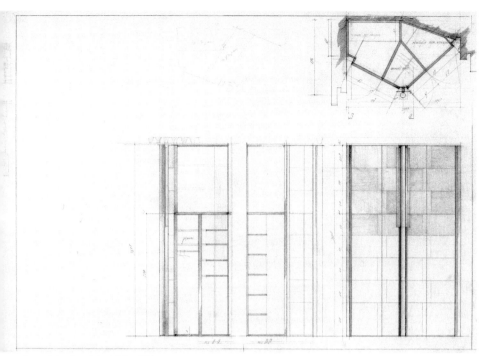

n, section, and elevation of closet, 1:10, c. 1982
aphite on translucent paper, 70 × 90 cm. ARCH271174

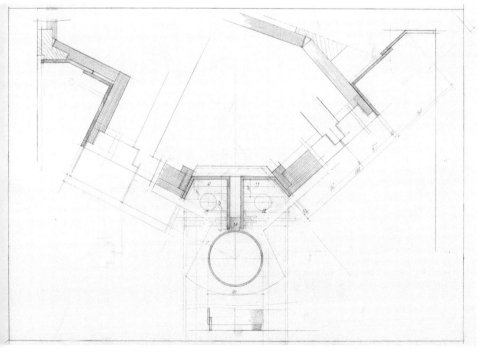

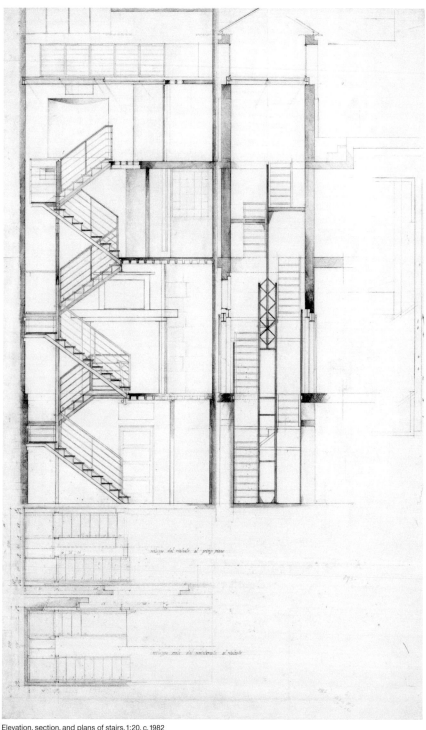

Elevation, section, and plans of stairs, 1:20, c. 1982
Graphite on drafting film, 97.1 × 60.2 cm. ARCH271189

case and skylight, c. 1984

First-floor office, c. 1984
Gelatin silver print, 30.64 × 23.5 cm. Photograph by G. Chiaramonte

dowsill in living room, c. 1984
atin silver print, 30.64 × 23.5 cm. Photograph by G. Chiaramonte

Veranda in rear garden, c. 1984

> Section and elevation of veranda, 1:10, c. 1982
Graphite and stamp pad ink on translucent paper, 88.1 × 59.9 cm
ARCH271154

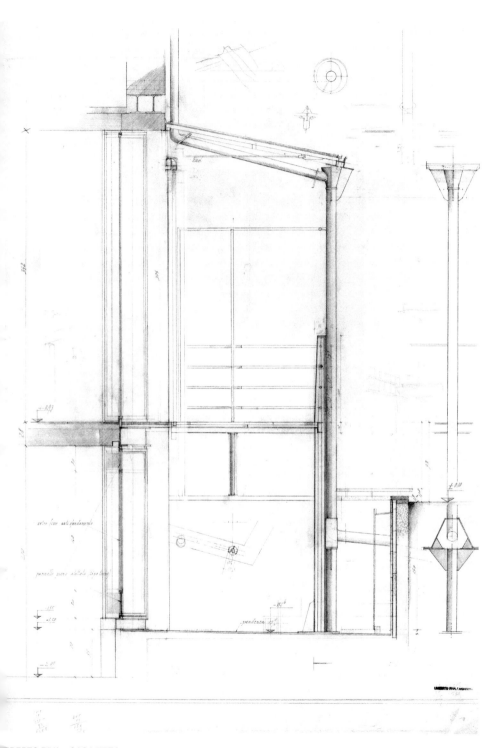

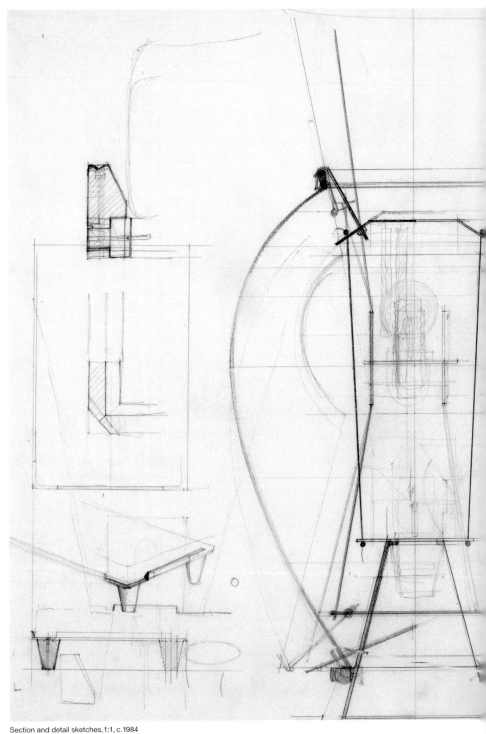

Section and detail sketches, 1:1, c.1984
Graphite on translucent paper, 60.48 × 93.19 cm

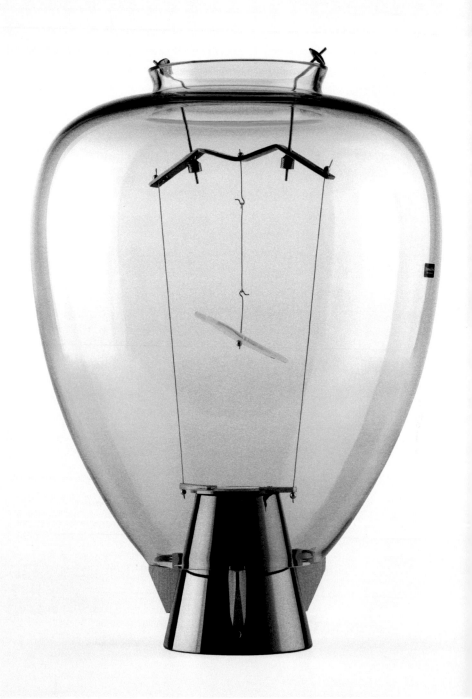

Green Veronese, 1985
Glass and brass, 50.8 × 37.19 cm × 37.19 cm. Photographs by CCA

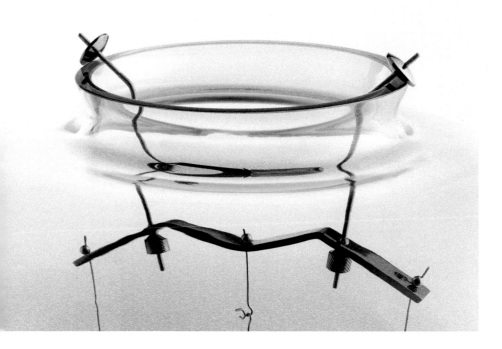

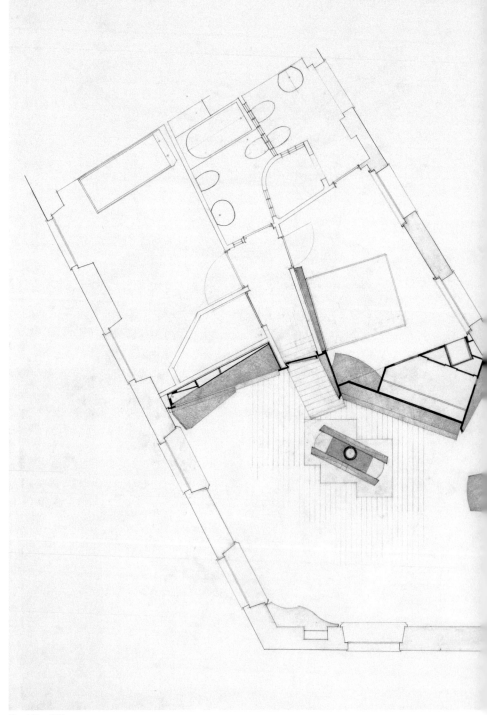

Plan, 1:20, c. 1987
Graphite on drafting film, 83.6 × 121.2 cm. ARCH271115

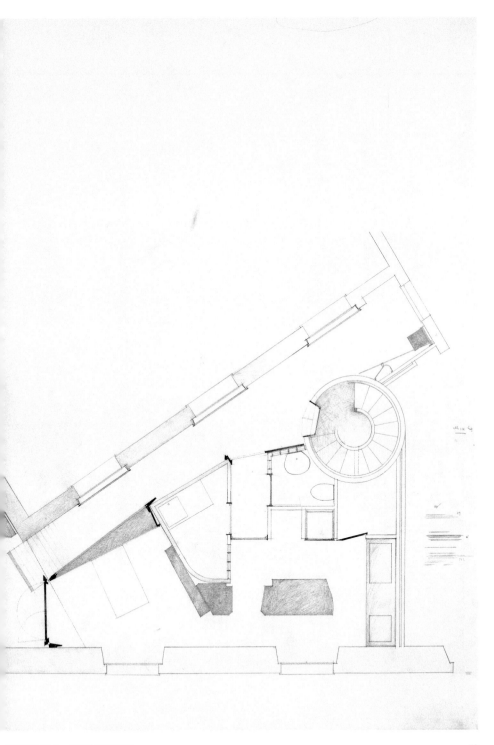

Views of corridor between entry and living room, 1990
Photographs by G. Chiaramonte

View from kitchen toward living room, 1990
Photograph by G. Chiaramonte

w from living room toward entry, 1990
otograph by G. Chiaramonte

Views of side table in kitchen and extendable table in living room, 1990
Photographs by G. Chiaramonte

> Details of side table in kitchen, 1:10 and 1:1, c. 1987
Graphite on translucent paper, 61.2 × 101.8 cm. ARCH271119

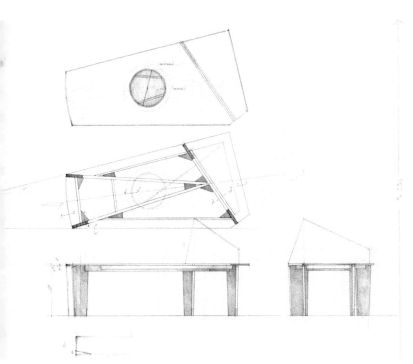

ns and elevations of living room table, 1:10, c. 1987
aphite on translucent paper, 53.4 × 61 cm. ARCH271123

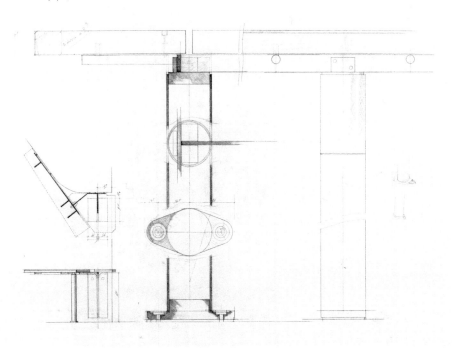

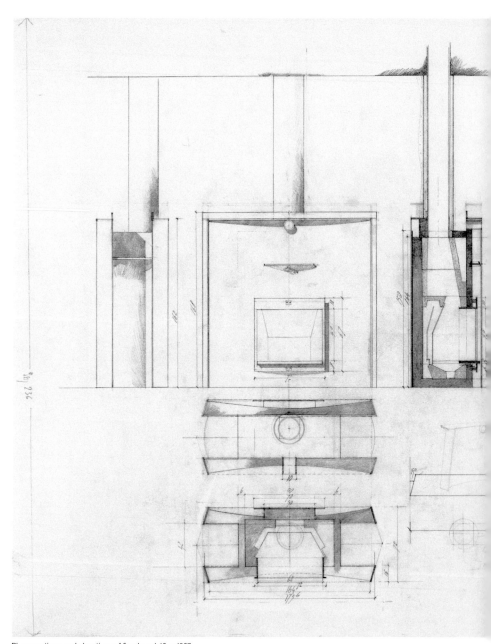

Plans, sections, and elevations of fireplace, 1:10, c. 1987
Graphite on translucent paper, 60 × 106 cm. ARCH271120

ews of living room showing fireplace and oak shelving, 1990
hotographs by G. Chiaramonte

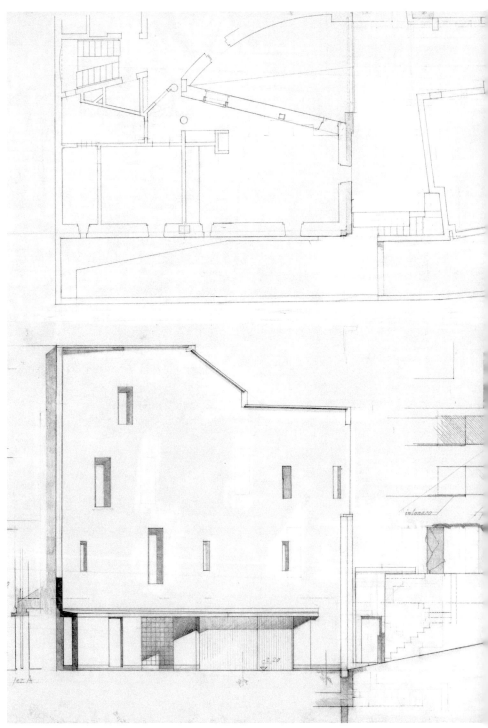

Partial plan of ground floor level and elevation of west facade, including view of courtyard, 1:10 and 1:50, c. 1992
Graphite on translucent paper, 60.9 × 84.3 cm. ARCH271112

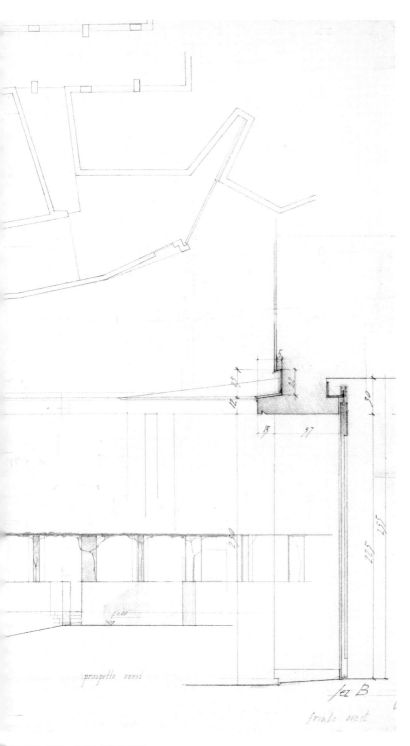

prospetto ovest

prospetto ovest

fronte ovest

/ez B

View of south facade from street, c. 1996

w of south facade from neighbouring building, c. 1996
ïtograph by G. Chiaramonte

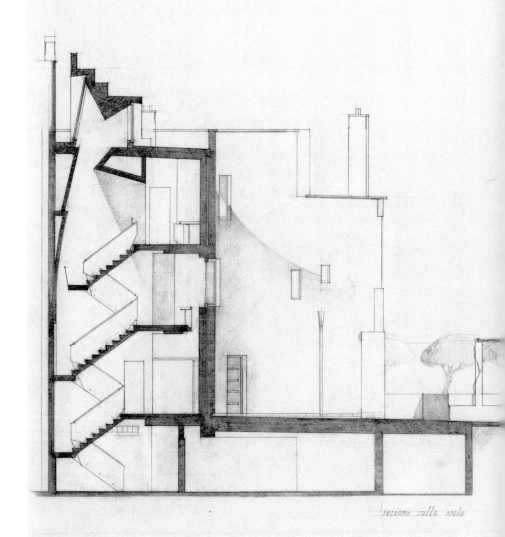

sezione sulla scala

Sections taken at stairs and through eastern volume of building, 1:50, c.1992
Graphite on translucent paper, 60.9 × 84 cm. ARCH271113

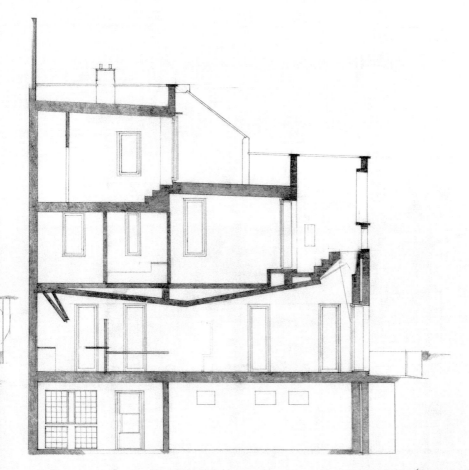

*sezione sul soggiorno*

View through pergola to cut in south facade, c. 1996
Photograph by R. Collovà

enings in south facade onto upper-level terraces, c. 1996
otograph by G. Chiaramonte

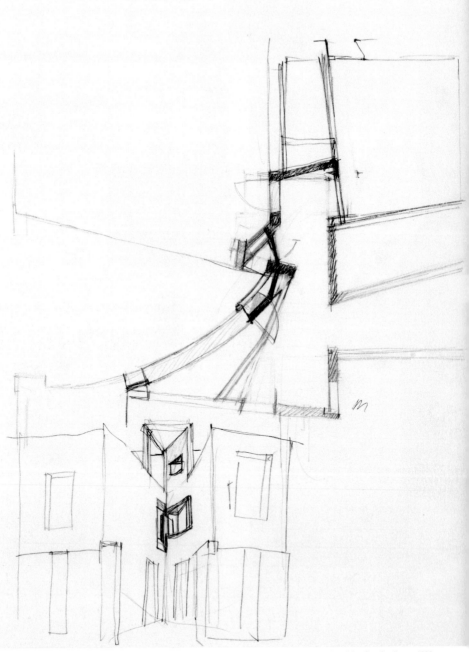

Early plan of first floor and perspective sketch of courtyard, c. 1992
Graphite on translucent paper, 44.6 × 30.7 cm. ARCH271098

> Views of stairwell and first floor landing, c. 1996

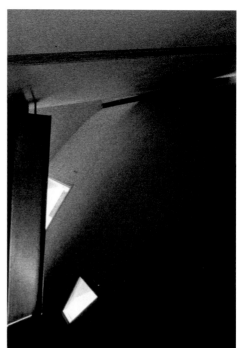

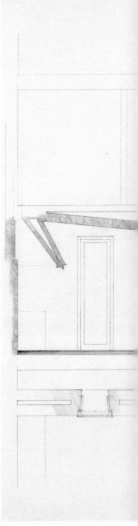

Views of living room and entry, c. 1996
Photographs by Monica Manfredi

Section of ground floor at living room,
1:20, c.1992. Graphite on translucent pa
60.9 × 83.9 cm. ARCH271109

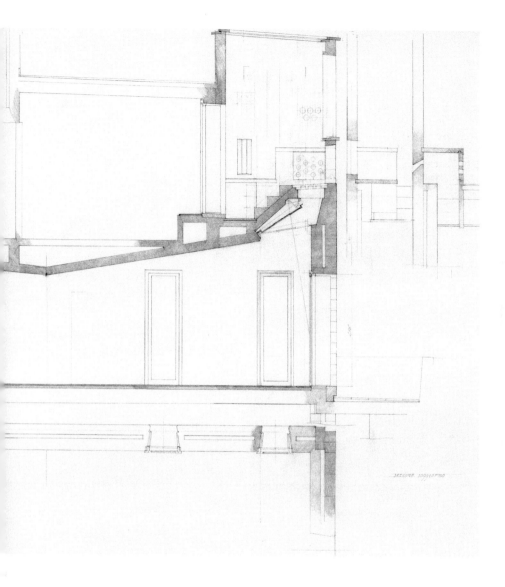

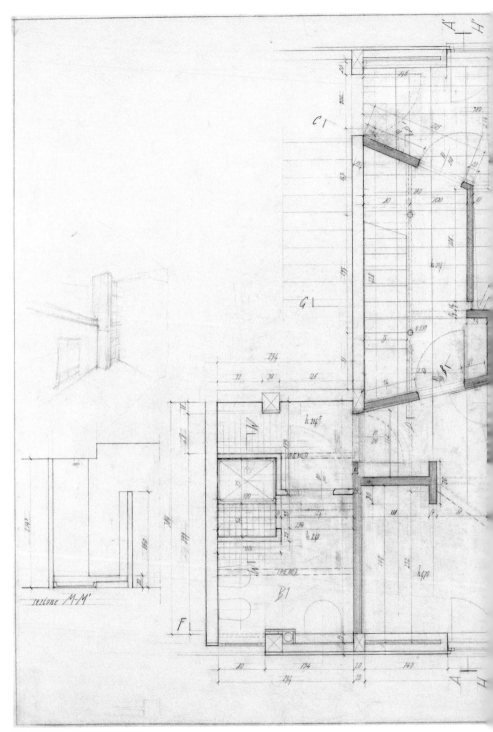

sezione M-M'

Plan of ground floor, 1:20, 2 August 2002
Graphite on translucent paper, 60 × 87.3 cm. ARCH271086

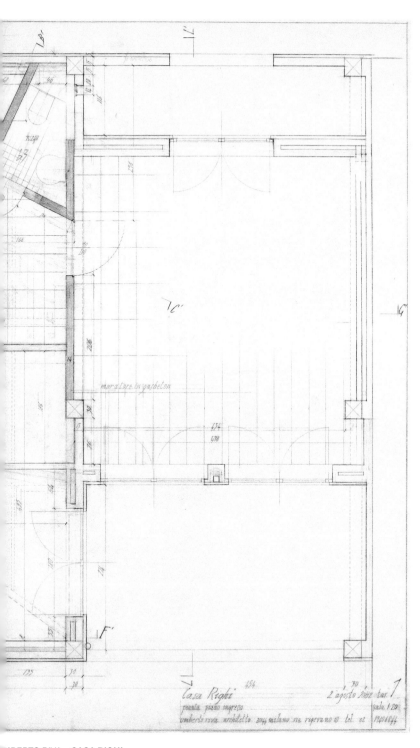

Casa Righi
pianta piano ingresso
umberto riva architetto 20... milano via rigevano 10 tel 02 ...

2 agosto 2002 tav. 1
scala 1:20

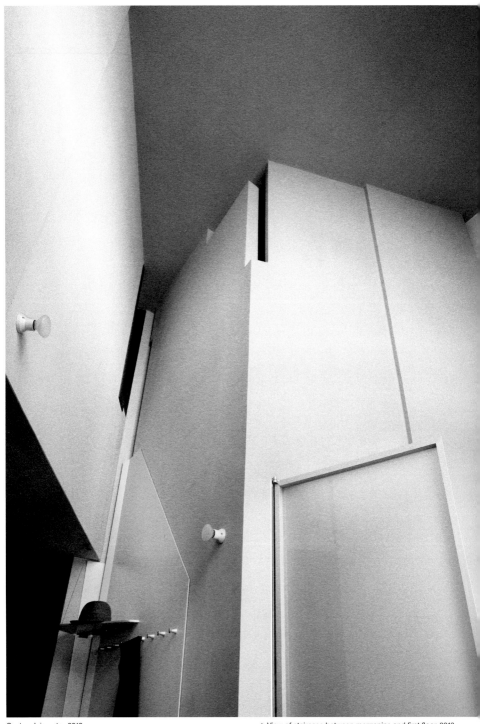

Coat rack in entry, 2013
Photograph by S. Caleca

> View of staircase between mezzanine and first floor, 2013
Photograph by S. Caleca

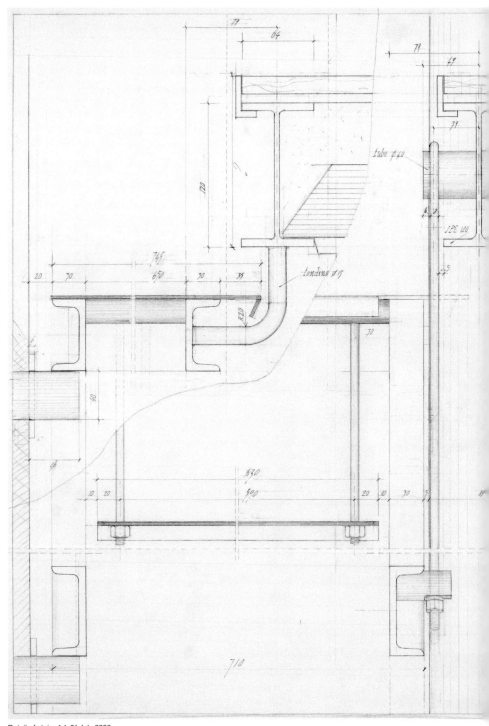

Detail of stairs, 1:1, 31 July 2002
Graphite on translucent paper, 60 × 91.8 cm. ARCH271092

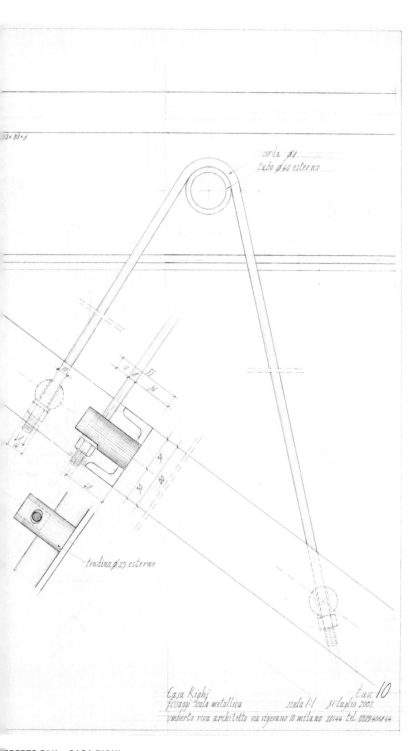

50×80×6

corda ø1
tubo ø40 esterno

tenditore ø25 esterno

Casa Righi
fissaggi scala metallica        scala 1:1    31 luglio 2002
umberto riva architetto via vigevano 10 milano 20144 tel. 0289406844

t.av. 10

Bedroom on mezzanine, 2013
Photograph by S. Caleca

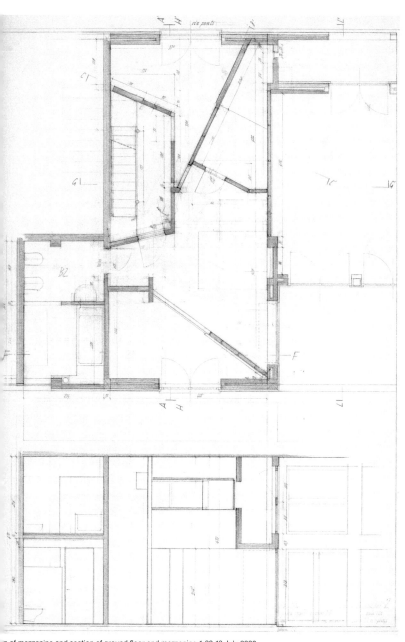

Plan of mezzanine and section of ground floor and mezzanine, 1:20, 13 July 2002
Graphite on translucent paper, 89.6 × 60 cm. ARCH271087

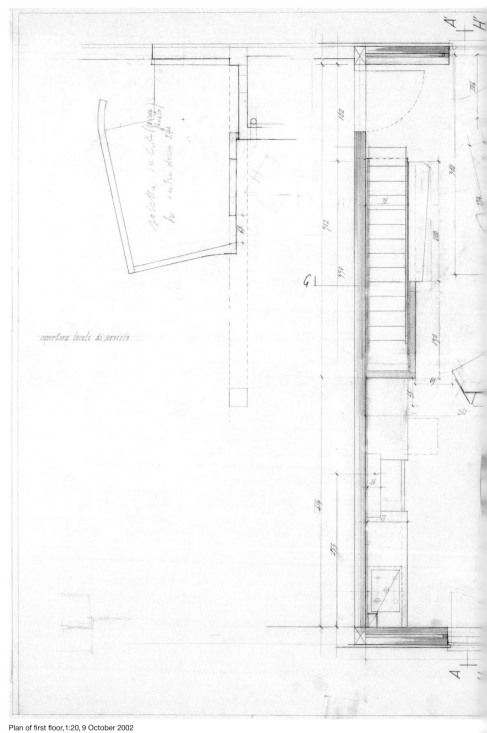

Plan of first floor, 1:20, 9 October 2002
Graphite on translucent paper, 60 × 92.9 cm. ARCH271088

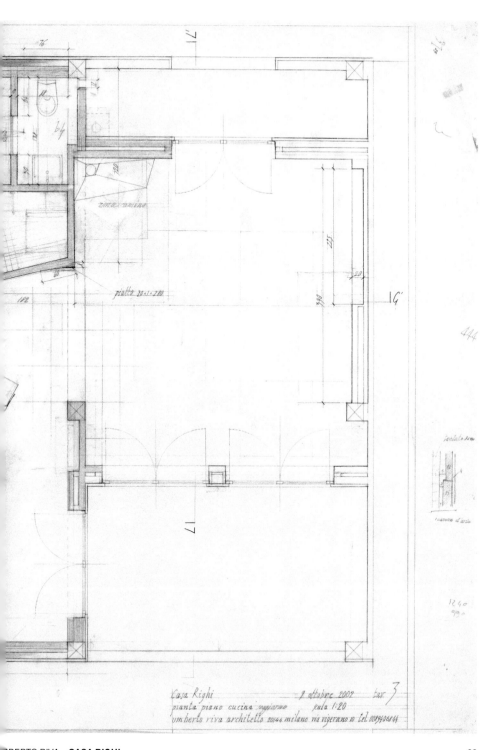

zona cucina

piatto 70.1.200

225

340

120

IG'

182

88

76

17

17

444

bocchetta presa

recuperio d'aria

1240
q/g°

Casa Righi                    9 ottobre 2002    tav 3
pianta piano cucina soggiorno      scala 1:20
umberto riva architetto 20144 milano via vigevano 10 tel. 0289406144

Views of first floor toward kitchen and toward living room, 2013
Photographs by S. Caleca

# UMBERTO
# RIVA

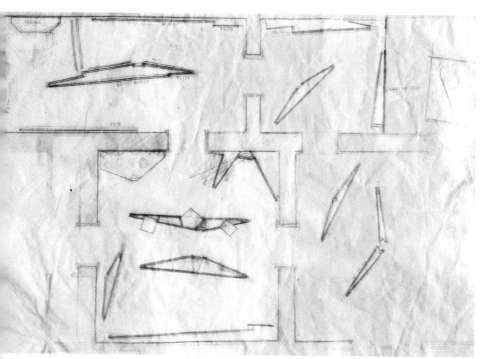

ch of installation design for the CCA galleries, June 2014

In Montreal, 28 February–5 March 2015

Photographs of *Rooms You May Have Missed*
by Giovanni Chiaramonte

111

Maybe we should change our viewpoint. We could look at what we commonly consider to be the production of contemporary architecture, whether buildings or projects, in the same way that Gilles Clément observes the animal and vegetable world. Clément searches for residual spaces: the remains of urban transformation projects, the scraps created by new infrastructure, the soil leftover from large tracts of farmland. It is in these spaces that the plants, insects, and animals that we cannot fit into our system of rational resource exploitation seek refuge. These locations become involuntary reserves, places for the reconstitution and redefinition of a biodiversity that perhaps, in the future, will be able to recolonize other territories.

If we were to look for similarly neglected spaces (understood also as spaces of incubation) in contemporary architecture, we would discover a much richer and more variegated panorama than we think is there. On European peripheries and in American suburbs, in South American and Asian metropolises, we would find folds, fractures, and points from which other practices and strategies—rediscoveries and reworkings of knowledge, methods, and materials; explorations that call into question the very notion of traditional architectural elements—might surface.

This is the case with Umberto Riva and Bijoy Jain. Riva challenges not only the usual organization of spaces but also the elements that make up those

Discussing the exhibition in Umberto Riva's office, Milan, January 2014
Photograph by CCA

spaces—doors, windows, walls, stairs, fireplaces— through a process of continuous dissection, in order to discover a new rationale for their existence, or transform them into something else. In Jain's work, alongside the reinvention of a local architectural culture, we find a proposal for alternative processes of designing and constructing buildings, as well as a redefinition of the roles of those involved: clients, builders, artisans, architects.

These are some fragments of a new, possible way to think about and to create architecture, as it gradually emerges from the slow withdrawal into itself of the fluid and (at times) sparkling output of recent decades, and from the disintegration of the neoliberal illusion, crushed underneath the weight of its apparent success. It is a seemingly modest architecture, but it is also ambitious and unyielding in its objectives. Refusing to give up disciplinary research, it considers, at the same time, the demands and problems that come out of our everyday lives.

These *rooms you may have missed* (both the rooms created by Riva and Jain in the galleries of the CCA, the traces of which remain in Giovanni Chiaramonte's photographs, and the rooms in their buildings) gather pieces of and aspirations for a different future architecture. They also convey a desire for a domestic environment and a private life, in a moment in which both seem destined to disappear.

123

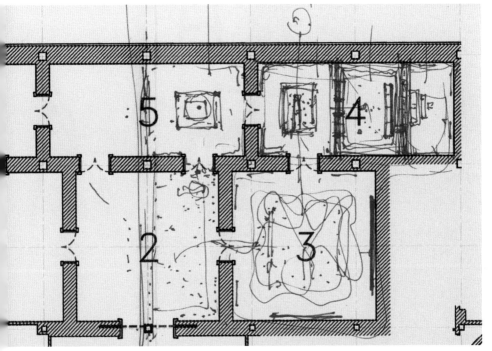

Sketch of installation design for the CCA galleries, May 2014

## Mumbai–Alibag

It takes a little over two hours by car to travel the one hundred kilometres separating Mumbai and Alibag, the village of twenty thousand on the Arabian coast that is home to Studio Mumbai. From the beginning of June to the beginning of September, during the monsoon, the ferry and catamaran service that links the Gateway of India in Mumbai with Mandwa Port, a few kilometres from Alibag, is interrupted.[1] Getting out of the city—in fact, a metropolis of more than twenty million inhabitants and the best representation of the transformations and contrasts marking contemporary India—means negotiating constantly gridlocked traffic. Thane Creek, the stretch of sea that isolates the peninsula of Mumbai from the mainland, has not stopped the city's breakneck expansion; the conurbation extends beyond it to Navi Mumbai, a new city built beginning in 1972 that has experienced such remarkable growth, particularly of the middle class, that its population at the 2011 census was 1.1 million.

Leaving behind the proliferation of office towers, residences, and malls that characterizes the landscape of Navi Mumbai today, the road begins to cut through thicker vegetation dotted with villages and occasional construction. This later gives way to an open countryside of rice fields; behind them, it is possible to make out the silhouettes of a few smokestacks and large industrial

1 The Gateway of India is a monument erected to celebrate the 1911 arrival of Queen Mary and King George V to the city that was then Bombay. The structure, a mix of Saracen-Moorish and Hindu influences, was not finished until 1924.

On the way from Mumbai to Alibag
Unless otherwise indicated, all photographs until page 166 by Mirko Zardini

plants. The conversation with Bijoy Jain and Mitul Desai, who works on some of Studio Mumbai's research and projects, is interrupted by a pit stop. A few dozen metres from the street, along a path and next to a low brick building, we see a series of structures covered entirely with layers of woven palm leaves, which— as Jain explains—are built as the monsoon approaches to protect the rice harvest. They are constructed by specialized artisans who periodically pass through the region between March and May, creating, repairing, altering, or completing these depositories as needed. This is not the first time that Jain has stopped to study these structures up close.

One might say that since his return to India, everything Jain has done has been based on this kind of observation. Sketches, photos, drawings, and notes about materials and details are all gathered in a series of albums, bound in red cloth, that we find over the next few days lining the shelves of his studio, open on the tables of his workshop, or at the construction sites of his buildings. These notebooks document cultivated fields, roofs of shantytowns, narrow passageways, lit parking lots, traditional buildings, water basins, trees, fabrics and canvases, shelters and temporary structures created for various festivals, bricks, stone quarries, heaps of gravel on the edges of construction sites, and buildings being demolished, which suddenly reveal, in a single image, the vibrant greens, reds, yellows, and blues of individual rooms. The red notebooks do not catalogue traditional elements; rather, they narrate Jain's fascination with spontaneous acts and conditions, discovered during trips throughout India, that manage to meet

Palm-covered structure to protect rice harvest; brick kilns

furniture; a little over a metre deep, they were created by the workshop's artisans using photos and reliefs of small cigarette stands and tailor shops in Varanasi, Kottayam, and Mangalore. The replica of the shop in Kottayam was prepared for the 2011 exhibition *Indian Highway IV*, curated by Hans Ulrich Obrist, at the Musée d'art contemporain in Lyon. In another part of the workshop there are models for wooden walls, furniture, and windows and doors among studies for other possible structures. In one corner lies a heap of minuscule bricks, which have just been fired in a traditional kiln; made to scale, the bricks will be used to create study models in the same material as the buildings themselves. On a stretch of bare ground, the rooms of the CCA, where Jain is preparing a part of the display for the exhibition *Rooms You May Have Missed*, have been traced with chalk. Three wooden pavilions host a laboratory of woodworking machinery, a large library, some shelves, and worktables lined with computers and the artisans' sketchbooks. In these, we find freehand drawings of windows, doors, walls, stairs, roofs—all at different scales, with measurements. The artisans' construction drawings develop in parallel to Jain's own sketches and the architects' drawings and models. Together, they are the site where the different groups within the studio discuss and verify various hypotheses and solutions, a fluid and continually updated internal mode of communication.

The variety of materials arranged around, above, and on the tables reveals a new way to conceive of architecture and its creation. Outside the workshop itself, Jain has reproduced these conditions

Studio Mumbai workshop; CCA gallery plan traced in chalk at 1:1 scale

is a kind of scenography—at the Venice Biennale, for example, and in an exhibition at Gallery MA in Tokyo, where replicas of the tables and materials (missing only the people) embody a manifesto for a renewed commitment to the senses, materiality, and artisanal knowledge. At Studio Mumbai, though, the objective is not only to define a new architecture capable of reinterpreting contemporary needs while incorporating local building traditions. It is also about a new way of working, one capable of redefining the process of planning and creating buildings as a collective act. Under the trees, we find students with laptops as well as carpenters, stonecutters, masons, electricians, woodworkers, and artisans specialized in brick, in plaster, in the use of colour. Each one participates in the elaboration of possible solutions in a process of collective research, discussion, and selection for which the architect—Jain emphasizes—acts as orchestra conductor, setting the fields of inquiry, orienting the studio's activity, and leading the search for the most appropriate solutions.

In the workshop that we've all come to know as Studio Mumbai, there are now typically two or three architects, some students, and about twenty artisans. The concept started to take shape a few years after Jain's return to India, in 1995, and really came together in 2000 in Alibag, when the workshop grew to around a dozen architects and one hundred artisans (ultimately peaking at two hundred). First, there were a few buildings constructed around Alibag—Kapoor House in Murud and Kapadia House in Satirje, completed in 1998 and 1999 respectively—with the collaboration of a group or six or seven craftsmen. These early projects gave

"Reading room" addition; Utsav House

rise to the idea to organize both the design and realization of his projects under a new, shared structure—an arrangement that is now entering a new phase. The number of architects and artisans involved has been reduced in recent months; this will facilitate the return of the workshop to Mumbai, in the new complex of Saat Rasta, now in the final stages of construction, and in another laboratory that will open nearby. A small outpost will remain in Nagaon but in a new location.

In recent years, the success of Studio Mumbai has brought numerous jobs outside of India. New buildings are now in the design or construction phases in Spain (a vacation house near Barcelona, part of a larger project; other participants include Office KGDVS, MOS, Johnston Marklee, and Sou Fujimoto), in France (the transformation of a convent into a hotel in Nice), in Onomichi, Japan (a project that converts part of a holiday resort village into a community centre, with a theatre, restaurant, bar, some hotel rooms, a tea house, and a gallery), and in Switzerland (a few houses on Lake Zurich). The practice and the identity of Studio Mumbai are changing in turn.

## Wood, stones, bricks

Not far from the laboratories, canopies, and pavilions, hidden among the trees, we find the house where Jain lives. It is a traditional building with an addition, built in 2003, wedged under the branches of a fig tree. Extending the incline of the existing roof, Jain created a bedroom-studio-reading room on the first floor and a porticoed space on the ground floor to act as an expansion

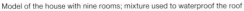

Model of the house with nine rooms; mixture used to waterproof the roof

f the kitchen. It is a modest-looking building—the necessity of ringing modesty and humility to the job is a recurring theme in onversations with Jain—that adapts to the existing house, ncorporating itself into and completing it. The new construction ppears as a transformation or evolution of the existing one, ne plastered masonry giving way to the new wooden structure and ne white, semitransparent agricultural netting that envelops it. eated in the room upstairs, we find ourselves suspended, protected :om and at the same time steeped in the presence of the trees, vhile a breeze from the garden passes through the netting.

'he extension of the house in Nagaon is the first in a series of rojects carried out since 2003 in the region surrounding Alibag, eachable by car in an hour or an hour and a half. To the south, bout thirty kilometres away in Kashid, near the sea, is Tara House 2005). Continuing for another ten kilometres along the coast, we rrive in Nandgaon, where, in the middle of a plantation of coconut rees, we find Palmyra House (2007). If, instead, we go north, we each Belavali House (2008), and then Utsav House (2008), which vas constructed for a software engineer in Satirje, about fifty ilometres from Alibag. Here, a series of stone walls protects garden surrounded by a few pavilions, which remind us, in their reakdown of vertical and horizontal planes, of Jain's time spent ι California.

ontinuing along the unpaved road, we slowly climb a hill that :ts us look over the surrounding landscape until we reach a house :ill under construction: nine rooms around a sequence of small

use with nine rooms under construction
otograph on right by Studio Mumbai

courtyards. People of all ages work on the site. Some are preparing tubs of lime that will be used in making plaster. Others are levelling the ground or laying the stone paving for the terrace that faces west, toward the countryside below. To one side there are piles of irregularly coloured bricks, which are usually thrown out because they are considered unusable. Some workers are preparing a special substance for waterproofing—a thick, shiny black mixture made from stones and oil—that has already been applied to portions of the roof. The same material fishermen have used for centuries to treat the bottoms of their boats is now being experimented with to cover buildings.

If we were to visit these houses in the order of their construction rather than their geographic locations, we would notice a reduction in the number of materials, a more regular floor plan, and a progressive simplification of details and architectural processes. The use of wood, so prevalent in the first projects, is more and more limited to the structure of the roof, the doors and windows, the verandas, and the porticoes, while the use of brick is more apparent. Very often Jain relies on discarded or less-valuable materials; not only the bricks but also the stones and marble are accessible and affordable. This process of reduction is also evident in the roofing; the copper sheets of Copper House II give way to black coating, which, at the house with nine rooms, descends to cover the highest strip of the brickwork until it meets the grey plaster.

Well on site of Copper House II during construction; pool near Studio Mumbai workshop
Photograph on left by Studio Mumbai

# rooks, rain, basins, wells

nlike the new constructions that dot the coast and surrounding
ills, whose claims to uniqueness make them banal, these
ouses are constructed with the same materials that we find in
ne homes of artisans and farmers flanking the road. In the
ardens or courtyards of Jain's projects, we find not typical
wimming pools but wells and basins that recall similar structures
sed to collect water and irrigate fields. Even the colour of the
rater is different: not an intense azure but a pale green, a reflection
f the plants that surround the tanks or of the green marble that
nes them. Sometimes we can swim in these rectangular basins,
1st as Jain, drawing on his past as a swimmer, dives into the pool
idden among the trees next to the house in Nagaon each day.
ther times, as in Utsav House, these water basins host aquatic
owers and plants.

opper House II isn't far from the house with nine rooms. It was
onstructed in 2011 as a temporary residence for a couple who
itended to spend a few days each week away from the chaotic
hythms of Mumbai. Dusk has fallen when we arrive. What at
rst glance seems to be a lush and inviting landscape is actually
ense, even claustrophobic; within this vegetation the house
tands solidly, repelling the incessant growth of flora outside its
ralls. In fact, the soil gathered from the excavation of the site
ras used to create a slight embankment on which the house sits,
levated above the surrounding ground. At the house's core is
rectangular courtyard, a small, protected enclave allowing views
f the sky. Around this slender courtyard, the living spaces are

of, Copper House II
otograph on right by Studio Mumbai

arranged one after another under a series of triangular wooden trusses. There are no corridors; the inhabitants criss-cross the courtyard unless the rains force them to take cover under the roof's inward-pointing eaves.

Later, we find this tapered roof detail again, drawn at a 1:3 scale on the tables of the workshop in Nagaon and leaning on a wall at the construction site for the Saat Rasta project in Mumbai. Etched with pencil onto a sheet of flexible, four-millimetre-thick plywood (used for packaging material, for example), the section is conjured in white tape carefully placed by the carpenters. At Copper House II, the roof's surface—a material treatment which would be impossible to duplicate given its current market value—caps the home tightly and engulfs the two kitty-corner volumes on the upper level that contain the master and guest bedroom suites. Even at this height, the foliage is overwhelming, but the offset volumes still manage to offer views of the surrounding landscape, not out but rather over—by pushing the jungle away.

If we leave the house and advance into a grove of mango trees, we find a well and a pool, small pockets of relief from the green. The presence of water in the area is not without its disadvantages, though; it can also be menacing. During the monsoon and par-ticularly intense rainstorms, a nearby brook can overflow and flood the surrounding land. The slope toward the brook is almost imperceptible: on one side, by the living room, a few steps descend to the garden, while on the opposite side, at the entrance, the land gradually rises. Along its perimeter, the rock paving

Embankment and landscape, Copper House II
Photograph on left by Studio Mumbai

f the embankment creates a sort of plinth on which the building tands. When the brook overflows, the house perches on its rotected island while the water invades the garden.

ack in the courtyard, Jain mentions a house in Chennai, still 1 the planning stage, that also grows out of and develops around ie idea of water. The design is organized around a courtyard ccupying the lot's centre, shaping a green band between the build-1g and an existing wall around the site. The house will be built ith stone slabs, using lime and wood for the shingles, in a grid f 4.2 by 4.2 metres that references the architectural typologies f the region. The entire construction is conceived as a mechanism )r the collection and distribution of water. Water will be pumped 'om a well at the centre of the courtyard to the roof of the building very day and then released to flow over the shingles, reproducing )r anyone inside the house a similar effect to the rain pouring ver the roof of the house where we are now. The water will also ow along the surrounding wall, ultimately irrigating the soil. 1 this way, the relationship between the house and the perimeter 'all creates a microclimate that encourages vegetation to thrive. 'he designs already indicate which plants and flowers should row around the house: pineapples and pink bananas, elephant ear, ueen of the Night, papyrus, star jasmine, torch ginger, and so on.

**he domestic landscape: the courtyards**

Iany of Jain's dwellings are structured around a courtyard. )metimes it is only hinted at through the juxtaposition of volumes, s in Leti 360 (2007), in the foothills of the Indian Himalayas, or

sting wall around site and sketch of vegetation and site organization, house in Chennai otograph and sketch by Studio Mumbai

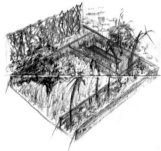

at Palmyra House; both projects comprise two buildings that shape a long and narrow space oriented toward the landscape or the sea. Other times, like at Tara House, a continuous roof links the different buildings, creating a central, if irregular, space. Slowly, Jain's courtyards have come to assume a more defined form; in Copper House II, for example, we find a paved, rectangular space that is no longer composed of different elements, but rather almost hollowed out from a volume. This is even more evident in the house in Ahmedabad, a brick building with a concrete frame whose design is equally indebted to local tradition and the modern monuments left by Le Corbusier and Louis Kahn. As we drive, Jain relates stories of childhood trips across India with his family and his strong—at the time disturbing—impressions of Le Corbusier's architecture in Chandigarh. The house in Ahmedabad, however, references both Le Corbusier and Kahn's work in its own city: the Sarabhai House, oriented to the prevailing winds, flanked to the southwest by a series of walled porticoes and made of brick and rough concrete; and the Indian Institute of Management, where the overwhelming, monolithic brickwork is pierced periodically to allow light and air deeper inside.

Built along what used to be called the outer ring road—the city now having far outgrown naming conventions established just a few decades ago—the house in Ahmedabad sits on a large, flat site that is home to a family of peacocks. (Jain's clients say the peacocks appear regularly at dawn and dusk, their heads poking just above the rooflines.) Intrigued by the pale-coloured ground, reminiscent of the sandy deserts of Rajasthan, Jain chose to use

Pressed-earth bricks on site, house in Ahmedabad
Photographs by Studio Mumbai

ompressed blocks made on site with the earth excavated to
ay the building's foundations. From the outside, the building
–or rather complex of buildings—appears as a low, sprawling,
nasonry-clad mass. Three two-story volumes anchor the central
ourtyard to the north, east, and west, allowing sunlight to pour
ver the south-facing portico near the entry. The brickwork is
otalizing, covering all exterior surfaces including the ground,
valls, stairs, and handrails of the walkways that connect the
edroom suites above. Occasionally, the masonry blocks are gently
ulled apart—a feat made possible by the concrete load-bearing
rame—so breezes can flow through the home while low early-
norning and afternoon light is filtered out. These single-width
creens, similar to the traditional wooden jali, are strategically
ocated near the covered exterior dining area and provide a degree
f privacy for the small gardens adjacent to the bedrooms. The
urge marble-lined pool in the middle of the courtyard slowly
vaporates throughout the day, tempering the traditionally arid
limate—an oasis. But unlike at Copper House II, the central court-
ard here is not the singular logic behind the home's organization.
maller courtyards in the three main volumes, each belonging to
different member of the extended family, and additional private
ourtyards create views of the surrounding landscape off each
f the bedrooms on the upper level. When the central courtyard
s filled with the forty or so guests the family entertains every
ther month, these volumes, along with the silhouettes of the
ller buildings beyond, create the impression of being in a small
own square.

urtyard, Copper House II; interior courtyard, Saat Rasta; passageway on upper level, house in Ahmedabad
otographs by Studio Mumbai

Despite their unitary appearance, Jain's buildings are actually very articulated. They gather under one roof, or in a single complex, different dwellings or residences that share spaces and communal services, such as the kitchen, loggias, and courtyards. When the house is not the primary residence, as is the case of many of the dwellings constructed near Alibag, the second home offers the opportunity for parents and children—or brothers and sisters, as in the case of the house with nine rooms—to gather together a few days each week or during certain periods of the year. The courtyard, the loggias, and the semi-open and semienclosed spaces that characterize the buildings emerge as the centres of a domestic landscape, protected from the intensity of the urban or natural environment—Mumbai's dense construction, the office buildings rising near the house in Ahmedabad, or the intense presence of trees and vegetation, as in Copper House II.

The relationship between the interior and exterior, and between the internal spaces themselves, is regulated through a sophisticated system of thresholds, passageways, and transition spaces. Verandas and porticoes, windows, adjustable shutters, and walls that fold back on themselves all offer the possibility of adapting to climactic conditions. At the same time, they allow for a great fluidity and flexibility in the use of spaces. From the very beginning, Jain's houses are conceived as a function of possible future conditions. The organization of each house and the articulation of its spaces are dictated more by the subtle modulation of transitions from private to increasingly public than by the definition of precise functions. We could think of these houses

Weavers' Studio site during construction; "woven vest" fabric produced by the textile studio
Photographs by Studio Mumbai

s schools, for example, without having to rethink their internal
rrangements.

## lace, time, energy

he Weavers' Studio, now under construction, is intended to
ccommodate a number of different uses in a series of separate
uildings, yet the complex's plan gives no sense of functionally
pecialized space. The studio is sited on high ground in Dehradun,
1 the agricultural region of Garhwal, a few hundred kilometres
orth of New Delhi. Three rectangular pavilions arranged in a line
efine the studio's northernmost limit and contain the residence
f Chiaki Maki, Jain's client and the studio's owner, as well as the
ome of the family charged with the site's upkeep and rooms for
isiting weavers and guests. To the west, a series of smaller pavilions
tep down the hillside and provide spaces for wet weaving and
yeing. The main weaving workshop is located in the largest build-
1g, a splayed rectangle which defines a pentagon-shaped central
ourtyard, a venue for the complex's social life; weather permitting,
1e looms can be moved outside as well. A smaller building farther
own the hill features a thin marble ceiling which glows during
1e day, backlit by four apertures that pierce the roof and stop just
hort of the stone. Goods produced in the surrounding buildings
ill be displayed here for sale. As a whole, the studio represents the
1ost extensive project to date for Jain and Studio Mumbai.

he plain below the workshop is punctuated by dwellings scat-
:red among cultivated fields; the project is driven by a close study
f this land, which had been abandoned for some years, and

rkshop building covered during monsoon and under construction, Weavers' Studio
otographs by Studio Mumbai

its potential. The building project is part of a wider environmental one, which envisions a recuperation of the land for the cultivation of indigo, silk, bananas, and, during the winter, sesame, among other plants. The arrangement of buildings is regulated by the tracks of irrigation canals and water flows. The materials—bricks and stones—are found on the construction site, or at most, a short distance away. The construction of the buildings has also followed both seasonal and agricultural rhythms. Building and weaving processes come together over a longer temporal cycle, integrating the succession and alternation of different types of work, from construction to agriculture to textile production. The project plan has thus become a kind of conversation with the surrounding world (physical, social, and economic), attentive to the possible lines of energy where the client's wishes, the architect's vision, the resources represented by the artisans' knowledge, and the resources offered by the context (whether material, temporal, or environmental) converge.

Among the architects that Jain cites as models for his approach and research—next to Geoffrey Bawa, the Sri Lankan architect known as a connoisseur of location, and Laurie Baker, the English émigré and proponent of sophisticated but low-cost brick construction, both of whom ably draw on local architectural traditions and the specificities of their respective tropical surroundings— Jain often mentions Robert Mangurian, his teacher at Washington University in St. Louis. The distance between Los Angeles, where Mangurian practices with Studio Works (with Mary Ann Ray), and Jain's India may seem unbridgeable, but the affinities between

Overgrown vegetation in existing building and unit containing Studio Mumbai office under construction, Saat Rasta
Photographs by Studio Mumbai

he practices are clear. From Mangurian and Studio Works, Jain earned not only to observe the world around him openly, without prejudice, but also and especially that the development of a project must strategize ways to capitalize on all available strengths and elements, even ones that seem less relevant.

## Alibag–Mumbai

The workshop's permanent relocation to Mumbai constitutes a new period in the evolution of Studio Mumbai. After years of research and experimentation in Alibag, the current desire is to put the experiences and methodologies they fostered to good use both in Mumbai and internationally. Just off the Saat Rasta roundabout and within walking distance of Dhobi Ghat, a new complex will soon house Jain's studio and home, along with three other units he plans to sell. Among his new neighbours are a lawyer and a publisher. The new complex sits adjacent to a railroad; on the opposite side, it faces a heavily trafficked road, which becomes even busier during the months of the festival in honour of Ganesh. The festival brings about the construction of temporary bamboo structures, inserted among existing buildings under improvised porticoes, which accommodate the work of artisans and vendors.

Jain's building is a former warehouse. After he discovered it in a state of disuse, he acted quickly to convert it before it was torn down to make way for a multi-story housing development. The oddities of the local building code—a remnant of colonial bureaucracy—dictated that the existing walls and footprint had to remain. The original A-frame roof, which spilled rainfall onto the adjacent properties, had to be replaced; runoff, however, needed to be managed on site. These constraints, along with Jain's recent projects in Chondi and Ahmedabad, clearly helped shape the plan. Deep overhangs ring ten rectangular courtyards that direct water not out, but in, to be collected in underground cisterns. The exterior brick walls have been rebuilt using debris found on site and topped with a new light steel–framed roof. Inside each unit, thin cement board partitions divide the spaces. The windows and furniture are teak, both made on site by carpenters under Jain's employ—and many will continue to work here, building prototypes for Jain's international commissions once Studio Mumbai's move is complete. Some units are organized around a single court, others two, and all are accessed along a central alley-way populated by the overgrown flora that Jain wanted to keep. Openings frame the lush vegetation, but the most notable views are of the sky: a deep, calming blue, rarely noticed in this most urbanized metropolis. At our backs, however, high-rise developments remind us that we are in a city of twenty-one million and not the mango groves of Maharashtra.

The project is not yet finished, and littered throughout we find the same materials that were arranged on the tables in Alibag: note-books with the artisans' sketches, large, thin plywood panels with details drawn at various scales, models, prototypes of windows and furniture for the kitchens, doorknob samples. Studio Mumbai has been a true laboratory; the buildings constructed until this point are like in vitro experiments, conceived in the protected

Tape drawings made by carpenters on site, Saat Rasta

nvironment offered by the new Indian bourgeoisie. Seated in the
ard, Jain recounts the different strategies Studio Mumbai has
mployed over the years: For some projects, such as Saat Rasta, for
xample, or Copper House II, or the house with nine rooms, the
ntire process—design development, on-site supervision and con-
truction—was (or currently is) managed by Studio Mumbai. In
he case of more complex projects or those further afield—like the
Veavers' Studio and the House in Chennai—Studio Mumbai makes
p part of a larger team including the client and contractor. A
ully integrated system requiring, at times, hundreds of carpenters,
nasons, and other artisans, has, with the increasing number of
nternational commissions, given way to a smaller office working
longside local partners. The vacation house outside Barcelona
night be seen as a midpoint in Jain's career; the project retains
 domestic scale and the rich tectonic quality for which he is
est known, but built in a foreign context with foreign tradesmen,
: represents a significant departure from his previous working
nethods. For the projects in France, Switzerland, and Japan,
he workshop still carries out its research developing designs,
naking sketches, and building models, which—often in segments
t scales approaching 1:1—become integral to the direction of
ne project and are utilized on site as references during construc-
on. For these projects, a new model of Studio Mumbai will
e created in each of the different locations, with local architects
nd artisans—a kind of Studio Onomichi in Japan, and so on.

he project in the small city of Onomichi and completion of the
aat Rasta complex in Mumbai are also preliminary steps in the

idy model showing possible modifications to chawl type; chawl housing in Surat
otographs by CCA (left) and Studio Mumbai (right)

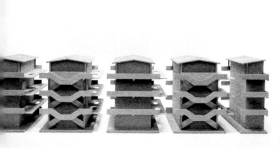

firm's attempt to deal with the urban scale. This wider focus, and especially the city of Mumbai, present new challenges for the office. The city's growth and radical inequality have been the subject of much scrutiny; 60 percent of the city's residents are housed in slums, and of the remaining 40 percent, three-quarters are living in poorly designed and cheaply built "chawls." Four to five stories in height, these tenement buildings often house families of six in a single room measuring less than fifteen square metres. An entire floor shares a common set of latrines. Daylight, space, water, and air are all in limited supply, but to advocate for the wholesale destruction of the chawls is to leave millions of the city's inhabitants without basic shelter.

In Alibag, just before leaving for Mumbai, Jain pointed to photos of the chawls and, next to them, study models of ways in which he envisions subtly transforming the building type. The studies articulate the possibility of larger openings allowing greater daylight to the interiors, wider balconies for the residents to gather, and more generous dimensions for the apartments—small interventions that acknowledge the tight tolerances that make the chawls economically feasible. "Where available space and resources are limited," the goal is straightforward: to transform these buildings into more hospitable places for their residents. Jain's materials-based research—the evidence of which currently covers the ground, tables, and shelves strewn throughout his studio in Alibag—is likely to continue, but the city he left over two decades ago demands new forms of research and equally innovative architectural responses.

Banganga public water tank, Mumbai

In mid-2015, Studio Works and Studio Mumbai will find themselves working together in Mumbai. Both, in fact, will be moving to the Saat Rasta complex—Mangurian and Ray for a limited time, although their visits will likely recur. Jain has long been fascinated by the water tanks in the heart of the city, and the offices will be jointly engaged in looking at these two-hundred-year-old construcions, once the city's only source of fresh drinking water. An attention to detail and the particularities of the country Jain calls his own will inevitably remain, but it will be interesting to see the city's influence—the energy of its dense disorder, its ability to meet "all basic requirements," its increasing global visibility— on the studio that took its name.

170 **WEAVERS' STUDIO**
Dehradun, Uttarakhand
2014–

184 **HOUSE IN CHENNAI**
Chennai, Tamil Nadu
2014–

194 **SAAT RASTA**
Mumbai, Maharashtra
2012–2014

208 **HOUSE IN AHMEDABAD**
Ahmedabad, Gujarat
2012–2014

220 **COPPER HOUSE II**
Chondi, Maharashtra
2010–2012

**WEAVERS' STUDIO**
Commissioned by Chiaki Maki, a Japanese textile weaver who spends a portion of each year in northern India, this complex in the Himalayan foothills provides working space for a studio of twenty-five weavers from all over the country. It is conceived as a cyclical, self-sufficient farm system that integrates all aspects of the weaving process, from cultivating indigo and henna for dye to gathering silk from cocoons and spinning wool. The site had been previously cultivated, and the design works with the landscape's existing pathways, terraces, and mango groves. Nearly all construction materials – including the brick, limestone, and phosphorescent river stones used in the foundation and to treat the brick walls – come from within a two-kilometre radius of the studio. Construction stops entirely during the monsoon.

The five-sided building occupying the centre of the site is the workshop itself, which frames a courtyard for gatherings (of weavers, children, etc.). A gallery in the complex displays the weavers' work, while the linear buildings accommodate motorcycle parking, a guest house, and residences for Maki and her partner as well as the site caretaker and his family.

**HOUSE IN CHENNAI**
Commissioned by a private equity investor in Chennai, a commercial hub on India's southeastern coast, this still-evolving design takes the form of a rectangular pavilion surrounding an open-air courtyard. The site is a former cricket pitch surrounded by a tropical garden.

The structure is in granite, a material commonly used in Chennai, paired with lighter materials such as brick and timber. To address the city's hot and humid climate, the house is conceived as a porous structure that allows free circulation of air and water. An integrated irrigation system carries water between the home's corrugated roof, its exterior walls, and a series of surrounding lotus ponds and gardens. This movement mimics the visual and cooling effects of a rain shower multiple times each day.

## AAT RASTA

Aat Rasta is a live-work complex in southern Mumbai that reuses the structure of an existing fire-damaged warehouse. Jain himself owns three of the six units—a residence, a studio, and a guest house.

The name of the project translates literally to Seven Roads, a reference to a nearby roundabout. The site is immediately adjacent to the Central railroad as well as an informal housing settlement, qualities which made the location undesirable for developers.

To adhere to zoning regulations, the design recoups the warehouse's original basalt stone perimeter wall. Brick infill delineates the units, while new wood-frame and cement-panel walls shape interior spaces. Each unit contains one or two courtyards, the roofs of which tilt toward to capture rain and avoid draining water on the surrounding housing. The courtyards also allow for the growth of local vegetation, especially Goolar figs, which had overgrown on the site before its redevelopment.

## HOUSE IN AHMEDABAD

Located on the developing periphery of India's fifth-largest metropolis, the house in Ahmedabad is the primary residence for an extended family that owns a power-generation facility in the state of Gujarat. Every other month, dozens of people come together at the house for social events, including family celebrations and business meetings. The gatherings take place in the courtyards that organize the project, which act as semipublic "interior" zones and generate much-needed shade in the hot, dry climate. A pool lined in green marble provides additional passive cooling, and local trees planted around the house will also retain water as they grow.

The house is constructed of concrete and earth bricks, which were made on site and pressed from the dry earth excavated to lay the foundation. This quick and economical technique is common in the Ahmedabad area and reduced damage to the site from construction vehicles, preserving a large population of peacocks living nearby.

## COPPER HOUSE II

Copper House II is the second residence of a couple from Mumbai, who visit the house for a few days each week. It is located in a dense grove of mango trees near a brook that floods each year during the monsoon. To protect the inhabitants from the encroaching landscape, the house is set on an artificial high ground made of dirt dug for a well from the site itself. The open-air courtyard at the centre of the plan is paved in black basalt stones that also allow rainwater to drain below the house.

On the ground floor, large horizontal windows are sheathed in slatted ironwood and copper mesh, providing a form of camouflage for the house while still permitting views out from the living spaces. The two boxy spaces upstairs are private: one contains a master bedroom and study, the second a smaller bedroom. The thin copper sheets that cover the upper floor are waterproof and will develop a verdigris over time, further concealing the house within its setting.

Contour model of site, 1:500, 2013
Wood, 18.6 × 65 × 71.1 cm. ARCH272109
Unless otherwise indicated, until page 233 all model photography by CCA
All other photographs by Studio Mumbai

View of site toward valley showing workshop under construction, March 2015
All photographs by Studio Mumbai are part of the CCA digital archive

Study models of workshop, 1:200, 2013
Wood, 4.1 × 21.5 × 17.4 cm. ARCH272114

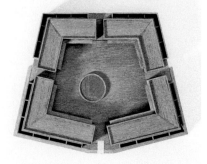

Wood, 3 × 21 × 16 cm. ARCH272113

Wood, 4.2 × 21 × 15.4 cm. ARCH272112

Wood, 4.5 × 20.5 × 16.8 cm. ARCH272111

Views of study model of workshop, January 2014

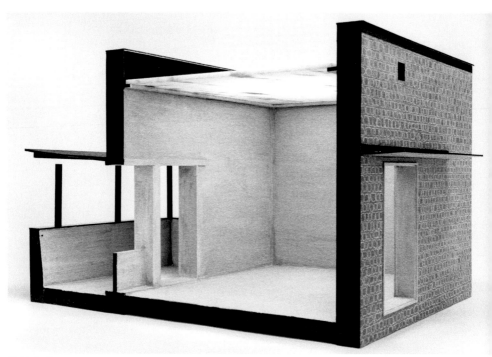

Model of gallery, 1:10, July 2014
Wood, paint, and marble, 50.8 × 87.63 × 59.06 cm. ARCH272110

> Gallery building under construction, April 2015

Study model of workshop, April 2014

> Brick samples treated with stone powder and lime mixture, April 2[

Views of complex under construction, April 2014–May 2015

Models of brick jali patterns, November 2013

Cleaning the bricks on the workshop building, January 2015

Study model, 1:300, 2013–2014
Wood, metal wire, and traces of graphite, 7.9 × 20.2 × 24 cm. ARCH272121

Study models, 1:300, 2013–2014
Wood and metal, 8.3 × 35.6 × 38.3 cm. ARCH272122

Wood with traces of graphite and pen and ink, 7.37 × 34.04 × 44.45 cm
ARCH272124

Wood, metal wire, and traces of graphite, 5 × 13.5 × 17.5 cm
ARCH272127

Wood and metal wire, 6.5 × 13.5 × 17.5 cm
ARCH272126

Wood with traces of graphite, 2.8 × 13.4 × 17.5 cm
ARCH272123

Wood, metal wire, and traces of graphite, 7.9 × 20.2 × 24 cm
ARCH272121

Wood and metal wire with traces of graphite, 5.2 × 19.5 × 28.2 cm
ARCH272125

Wood and metal wire with traces of graphite, 3.3 × 13.4 × 17.5 cm
ARCH272785

View of site with dimensions of project marked in chalk, December 2014

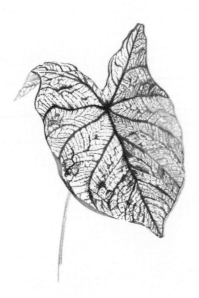

*Araceae – Candidum caladium* (Elephant ear)
Watercolour and graphite on paper, 41 × 31 cm. ARCH272133

*Commelinaceae – Rhoeo spathacea* (Oyster plant)
Watercolour and graphite on paper, 41 × 31 cm. ARCH272135

*Alismataceae – Sagittaria platyphylla* (Arrowhead). Coloured pencil,
watercolour, and graphite on paper, 50 × 35 cm. ARCH272136

*Bromeliaceae – Billbergia pyramidalis* (Foolproof plant)
Watercolour and graphite on paper, 41 × 31 cm. ARCH272134

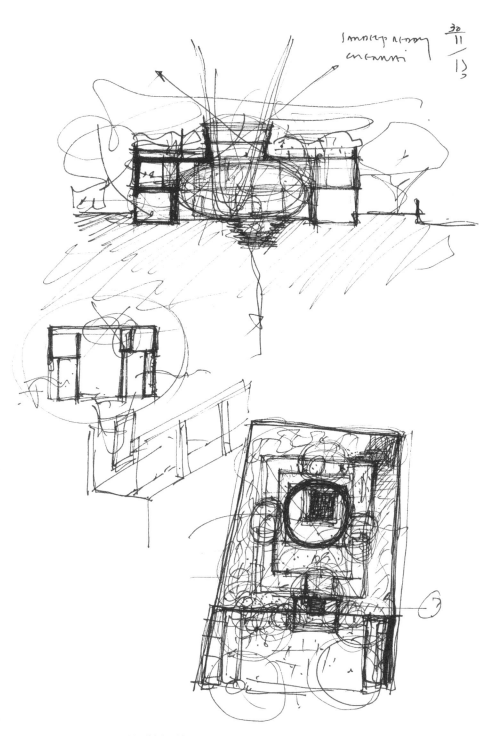

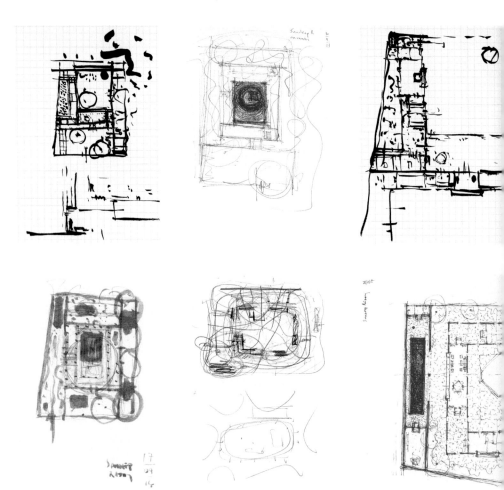

Schematic sketches by Bijoy Jain, August 2013–October 2014
CCA digital archive

> Plan sketch showing aqueducts and vegetation at night, October 20[
CCA digital archive

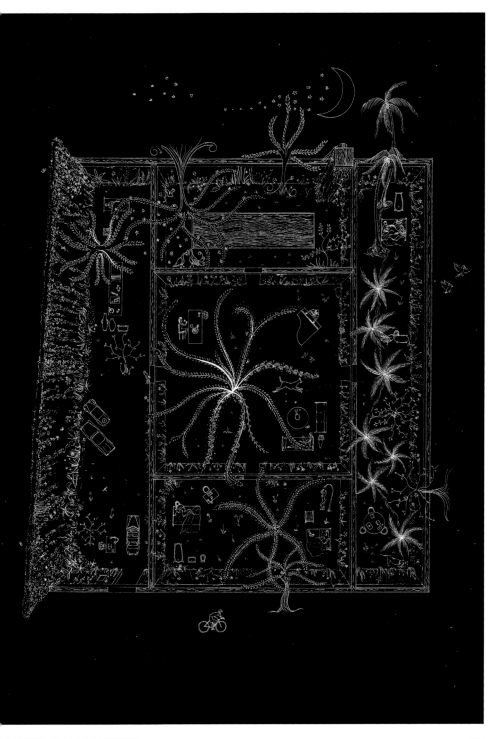

Presentation model, 1:198, July 2012
Bronze, 15.5 × 28.7 × 55 cm. ARCH272115

Aerial view of fire-damaged warehouse on site, 2009          > Aerial view and view from an interior courtyard, October 2014

Elevation of an exterior facade, 1:3, 2014
Pen and ink and graphite on masking tape on plywood, 154 × 283.7 × 0.8 cm. ARCH272128

Interior courtyard under construction, October 2014

Views of central passageway and interior courtyards, October 2014–February 2015

Stairs, bench, and interior courtyard during construction, September 2014

Interior courtyard under construction and central passageway,
February 2015

> Threshold onto interior courtyard during construction,
September 2014

Model of final design, 1:200, September 2014
Wood, graphite, dried plant matter, and paint, 8.89 × 45.72 × 26.67 cm. ARCH272116

East facade during construction, April 2013

Site during process of digging foundation, February 2012

Storage of pressed-earth bricks on site, April 2013

> Shed for making pressed-earth bricks on site, February 2012

Views of corridors and double-height courtyard, February 2014

Pressed-earth model showing volumetric organization of project, 2014
Photograph by Studio Mumbai

View of central courtyard facing north, April 2014

View of central courtyard facing east, April 2014

> Courtyard at entry to guest bedroom on upper level, April 2014

Study model, 1:192, December 2010
Wood, copper, and cardboard, 3 × 9.5 × 15 cm. ARCH272120

Study models, 1:192, December 2010
Wood and graphite, 3 × 7.5 × 13 cm. ARCH272117

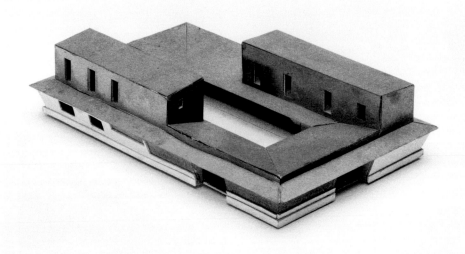

Wood, copper, and cardboard, 3.5 × 9.7 × 15.2 cm
ARCH272119

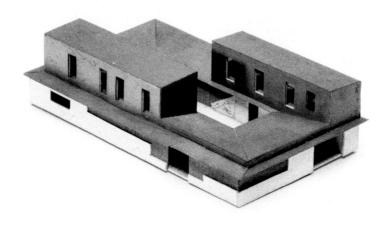

Wood, copper, and cardboard, 3 × 9.5 × 15 cm
ARCH272120

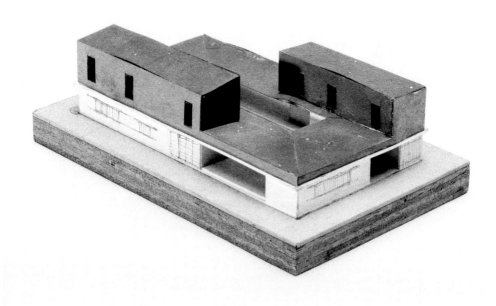

Wood, plywood, copper, cardboard, pen and ink, and graphite, 4.5 × 10.5 × 16 cm
ARCH272118

Window and ironwood screen, August 2012

> Stairway from upper level, August 2014

Courtyard, August 2012

> Northwest corner, August 2014; bridge over lily pond south of house, August 2012

BIJOY JAIN **COPPER HOUSE II** 227

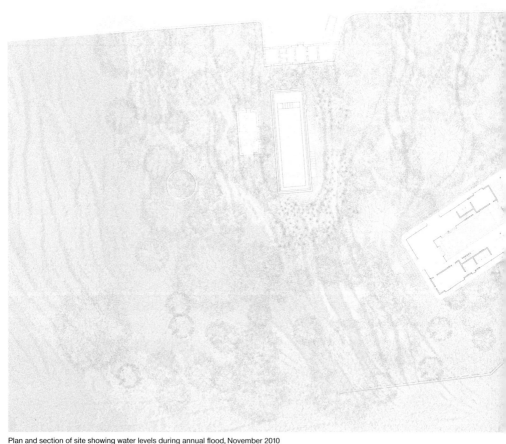

Plan and section of site showing water levels during annual flood, November 2010
CCA digital archive

Swimming pool and vegetation, August 2012

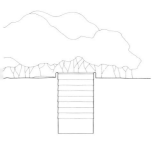

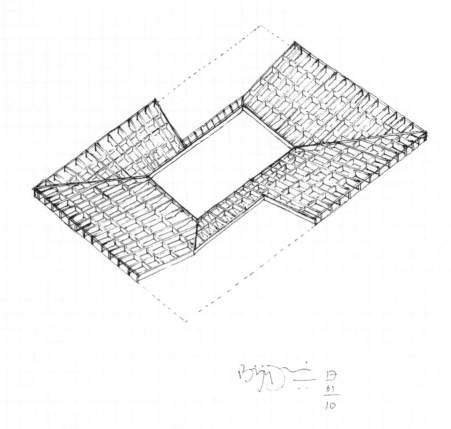

Bijoy ÷ $\frac{17}{01}$ $\frac{01}{10}$

PROJECT/ योजना अलिबाग खन्ना साइट (चौकि...)
DATE/ तारीख 10/11/09
DRAWN BY/ रचायिता प्रकाश सुथार.
DESCRIPTION/ वर्णन: ब्रिजोस फ्लोर रूफ स्कलर

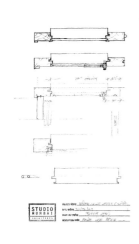

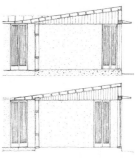

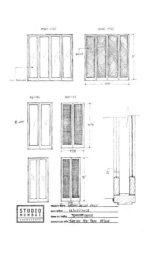

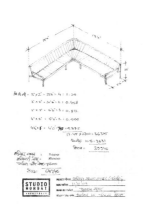

Roof and courtyard, August 2014

**MIRKO ZARDINI**

is an architect and has been Director of the Canadian Centre for Architecture since 2005. His research engages the transformation of contemporary architecture by questioning the assumptions on which architects operate today. After working with Giancarlo De Carlo and before coming to the CCA, Zardini led his own professional architectural practice in Milan and Lugano for over a decade.

Exhibitions by Zardini–or in collaboration with Giovanna Borasi–include *Asfalto: Il carattere della cittá* (2003), presented in Milan, and *out of the box: price rossi stirling + matta-clark* (2003), *Sense of the City* (2005), *1973: Sorry, Out of Gas* (2007), *Actions: What You Can Do With the City* (2008), *Other Space Odysseys: Greg Lynn, Michael Maltzan, Alessandro Poli* (2010), *Imperfect Health: The Medicalization of Architecture* (2011), and *Rooms You May Have Missed: Bijoy Jain, Umberto Riva* (2014), presented at the CCA in Montreal.

Editor of *Casabella* magazine from 1983 to 1988 and *Lotus International* from 1988 to 1999, Zardini served on the editorial board of *Domus* in 2004 and 2005. His research on the urban fabric and context of Italy and Switzerland resulted in the publications *Paesaggi ibridi* (Milan: Skira, 1996) and *Annähernd perfekte Peripherie* (Basel: Birkhäuser, 2001). His writings have appeared in journals such as *Lotus International*, *Casabella*, *ANY*, *Archis*, *El Croquis*, *L'Architecture d'Aujourd'hui*, *Domus*, *Volume*, and *Log*.

Zardini has taught design and theory at architecture schools in Europe and the United States, including Syracuse University, the University of Miami, ETH Zurich, EPFL Lausanne, the Università della Svizzera Italiana, Princeton University, and Harvard University.

**GIOVANNI CHIARAMONTE**

began his activity as a photographer at the end of the 1960s, working toward a return to figurative form after the abstract and *informel* tendencies of Pop and Conceptual Art during the twentieth century.

He has always devoted his attention to the relationship between place and man's identity. His most important works include *Giardini e paesaggi* (1983), *Terra del ritorno* (1989), *Penisola delle figure* (1993), *Westwards* (1996–2013), *Milan, The Rings of Middle City* (2000), *Dolce è la luce* (2003), *Like an Enigma. Venice* (2006), *Hidden in Perspective* (2007), *In Berlin* (2009), *L'altro nei volti nei luoghi* (2010–2011), *E.I.A.E. – Et In Arcadia Ego* (2012), *Interno perduto* (2012), *Piccola creazione* (2013), *Jerusalem* (2014), and *A medida do Ocidente*, with Álvaro Siza (2015).

Since 1974 he has exhibited in personal and collective shows worldwide, including at the Milan Triennale in 2000, 2009, and 2011 and at the Biennale of Venice in 1992, 1993, 1997, 2004, and 2013. In 2005 he was awarded an honorary degree in architecture by the University of Palermo. In 2010 he exhibited *Hidden in Perspective* at the Expo in Shangai. He has also founded and directed collections of photography for various Italian publishers.

Currently, he teaches the theory and history of photography at the Free University IULM and at the Nuova Accademia di Belle Arti (NABA) in Milan.

## UMBERTO RIVA

(born in Milan, 1928) has worked continuously as an architect and designer since 1959, when he graduated from the Università Iuav di Venezia. At the time, the school was directed by Giuseppe Samonà, who had assembled a group of influential instructors—Carlo Scarpa, Franco Albini, Giancarlo De Carlo, Bruno Zevi, Ignazio Gardella—and developed a design curriculum that emphasized *le esigenze umane,* or human needs, over rationalist abstraction.

Riva has rarely worked outside of Italy, and many of his early commissions were apartments and vacation homes for personal and professional contacts from Milan. Following the holiday home Casa Di Palma on Sardinia (1959), Riva's first major project was a housing complex on Via Paravia (1966), on Milan's western edges. Designed for a cooperative of friends and acquaintances that included Riva and his family, the building is a narrow, heavy block of exposed reinforced concrete punctuated by sets of rectangular windows and balconies carved out from its mass. Beyond additional homes for the Di Palma family on Sardinia and the Ferrario family in Osmate, Riva also designed the Casa Berrini on a hillside in Taino (1968), where a concrete "external" structure is pulled off a brick "internal" structure containing the living spaces.

Notable exceptions to Riva's early domestic work are the Bar Sem (1975), a renovated ground-floor bar demolished one year after it opened, and a school facility in Faedis (1979). Riva was asked to design this complex of primary and secondary schools as part of rebuilding efforts in the area near Udine, in Friuli, in northeast Italy, after a 1976 earthquake. The buildings are simple and linear, with almost-curved concrete-truss roofs, and were constructed traditionally rather than prefabricated.

By the mid-1980s, Riva entered his most significant phase of work, marked by the conversion of the townhouse Casa Frea. His experiments with the design of a glasshouse-like angular window were shown at the seventeenth Milan Triennale in 1986; in response to the theme of "domestic design," the window frame not only mediates how light and heat enter the home but also provides an unexpected formal break in the wall's flat surface. In 1987, he designed an unbuilt urban project for the city of Ancona. His approach to urban public space appears again in the Piazza San Nazaro in Milan (1989), where a geometric paving system subtly reshapes an existing square to accommodate the construction of a subway station.

Riva began designing lamps and furniture during his architectural studies, and these elements frequently appear within his interiors. His lamps, in particular, display his intensive attention to details and exhibit a characteristic mix of high and low materials, from wood and plastic to delicate, hand-blown Murano glass. His custom furniture frequently takes on an architectural role, framing and organizing the plan of a project and pointing to his observations of the smallest aspects of daily life.

Since the 1990s, Riva has also been active as a designer of exhibition spaces, including an office showroom in Padova (1992) and the Galleria AAM Architettura Arte Moderna a Milano (1997). He has designed installations for exhibitions on John Soane (Palazzo Barbaran da Porto, Vincenza, 2000; CCA, Montreal, 2001), Carlo Scarpa (Palazzo Barbaran da Porto, 2000), and Le Corbusier (MAXXI, Rome, 2012), among others, as well as his portion of the CCA exhibition *Rooms You May Have Missed: Bijoy Jain, Umberto Riva* (2014).

He continues to work in Milan.

**BIJOY JAIN**

(born in Mumbai, 1965) comes from a family of doctors, a profession he was determined not to pursue. Architecture was an intuitive choice, and after a few years in architecture school in India, Jain moved to the United States to continue his education.

In 1990, Jain received a Master of Architecture from Washington University in St. Louis, where he studied under Studio Works founder Robert Mangurian. He worked in the model workshop of the architect Richard Meier in Los Angeles until 1991; Mangurian, who is also based in Los Angeles, continued to act as a mentor. Jain then formed a small firm in London with a colleague from Meier's office before returning to a rapidly industrializing India in 1995.

Jain's experience acclimating to India's economies of construction after his time abroad was a significant factor as he shaped his first individual practice, Bijoy Jain Associates, in Nagaon, outside Mumbai. In designing his initial residential commissions, such as the Kapoor House (1998), Jain explored and ultimately refined a way of working that incorporated the knowledge of a team of traditional craftsmen and tradesmen, particularly through the use of iterative and often full-sized scale models. "Despite the fact that I was trained in an academic and professional environment dominated by modern ideology, once I was back in India I started to be really fascinated by local architecture. But this wasn't a case of nostalgia," Jain explained in an interview in 2012. "Collective working practices became very important in themselves."[1]

Many of Jain's projects are houses built outside Mumbai or in other major cities for members of India's rising elite—software developers and finance professionals, for example. As with Jain's later designs, his early homes exhibit a sensitivity to landscape and climate and a volumetric approach to composing space, with rooms frequently arranged around a central courtyard. The "reading room" (2003), an addition to an existing house, wraps a teak frame with white mesh netting commonly used in agriculture; the enclosed extension it creates remains permeable to light and air. The slatted-wood surfaces of Tara House (2005) are organized in a notched oval surrounding an aquifer, which provides fresh water for gardens and a swimming pool.

Jain founded Studio Mumbai in 2000 with many of the craftsmen who had been working with him since his return to India, and built an open-air workshop compound in Alibag. The organization and methods of the workshop itself have become important aspects of the practice's identity; an award-winning working mock-up of the studio, entitled *Work Place*, was exhibited in the Arsenale at the Venice Biennale in 2010. Other significant installations by Jain include a plaster-cast scale reproduction of an informal settlement in Mumbai created as part of the exhibition *1:1: Architects Build Small Spaces* at the Victoria and Albert Museum in London (2010).

In addition to his design work, Jain is active as an educator and lecturer, and has held teaching positions at the Royal Danish Academy of Fine Arts, Yale University, and the Università della Svizzera Italiana. Although the majority of his work remains in India, projects such as META (2011), a pavilion for an earthquake-damaged coastal site in Tumbes, Chile, represent Jain's efforts to apply his mode of working to other economies and cultural contexts. The house with nine rooms, currently under construction in the village of Katalpada, represents an increasing interest in brick structures—another form of the adaptation that characterizes his approach.

Jain is in the process of moving the office to Mumbai itself, although he will keep a small atelier in Nagaon, near the Alibag workshop. He has recently been commissioned to build homes in Barcelona and Zurich, a converted hotel in Nice, France, and a renovated hotel and social complex in Japan.

1 "The True Sense of a Community: Interview with Bijoy Jain," by Francesco Garutti, *Abitare* 523 (June 2012), 48–49.

## ACKNOWLEDGMENTS

This book and the exhibition it accompanies reflect the Canadian Centre for Architecture's ongoing efforts to look at architecture from a number of different perspectives that explore broader economic, social, and political issues.

This project involved many people, and *Rooms You May Have Missed* is a product of their collaboration, expertise, advice, and support. First and foremost, I would like to thank Bijoy Jain and Umberto Riva. This project would have been impossible without their committed participation throughout the lengthy process—involving travels, site visits, and many discussions and proposals—that eventually led to the exhibition and this publication. I'm very pleased that the material shown in the galleries has since entered the CCA's archives and is now resurfacing in the pages of this book, together with the expressive character of Jain and Riva's exhibition designs skillfully captured in Giovanni Chiaramonte's photographs. The exhibition's sophisticated graphic design was the product of Yoonjai Choi and Ken Meier's (Common Name, New York) creative insights.

My work—in Mumbai, Milan, and Montreal—would not have been possible without the help of Jain and Riva's close collaborators, among them Srijaya Anumolu, Mitul Desai, Lakshmi Menon, and Emilio Scarano. Their contributions, providing precious insights into Jain and Riva's working methods, were invaluable in the development of the exhibition and publication.

This book is also the result of many long discussions with Lars Müller. We are indebted to him and his office for their brilliant graphic interpretation of Jain and Riva's work.

Every CCA project requires the collaboration of a large part of the institution's staff. In particular, I would like to thank Giovanna Borasi for her constant support and constructive critiques; Delphine Lesage and Rebecca Taylor for their efforts in coordinating a dispersed team of international collaborators and contributors working from Milan, Mumbai, New York, and Montreal; Sébastien Larivière for his excellent work on the realization of the installations proposed by Jain and Riva; Albert Ferré for his guidance throughout the publishing process; Jayne Kelley for her editorial work shaping the texts and putting together the publication currently in your hands; Elliott Sturtevant for his research and ingenuity; and the CCA's Collection staff, particularly the Registrar and Conservation teams, for ably dealing with the large quantity and variety of material presented in the exhibition.

Finally, I would like to thank Phyllis Lambert, who supported the effort from the outset and recognized the exhibition's potential for reflecting upon novel attitudes toward the act of inhabitation in contemporary architecture.

Mirko Zardini, Director
Canadian Centre for Architecture

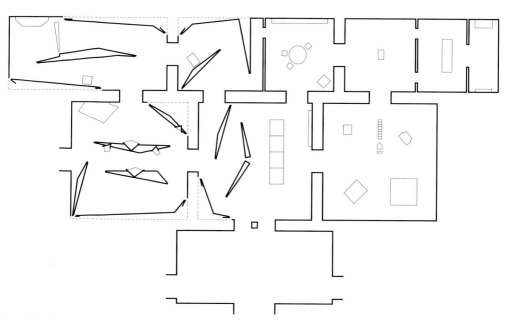

*Rooms You May Have Missed* combined gallery plan, October 2014. © CCA

This volume is published by the Canadian Centre for Architecture and Lars Müller Publishers in conjunction with the exhibition *Rooms You May Have Missed: Bijoy Jain, Umberto Riva*, organized by the Canadian Centre for Architecture, Montreal, and presented at the CCA from 4 November 2014 to 19 April 2015. It is also issued in French under the title *Des pièces à ne pas manquer: Umberto Riva, Bijoy Jain*.

This book is part of a CCA series that includes *Gilles Clément/ Philippe Rahm : environ(ne)ment : manières d'agir pour demain – approaches for tomorrow* (2006), *Some Ideas on Living in London and Tokyo by Stephen Taylor and Ryue Nishizawa* (2008), and *Other Space Odysseys: Greg Lynn, Michael Maltzan, Alessandro Poli* (2010).

Legal depot: August 2015

Printed in Germany
First edition

978-1-927071-14-4
Canadian Centre for Architecture
1920 rue Baile
Montréal, Québec
Canada H3H 2S6
www.cca.qc.ca

978-3-03778-458-7
Lars Müller Publishers
8005 Zürich, Switzerland
www.lars-mueller-publishers.com

**PUBLICATION**
Author: Mirko Zardini
Editor-in-charge: Jayne Kelley
Research: Elliott Sturtevant
Translation: Kimberly Ziegler
Proofreading: Katie Moore
Rights and reproductions: Marc Pitre
CCA photography: Michel Boulet, Mathieu Gagnon
Studio Mumbai photography: Srijaya Anumolu, Mitul Desai, Lakshmi Menon, Pedro Saraiva
Design: Integral Lars Müller/Lars Müller and Martina Mullis
Lithography: Ast & Fischer, Wabern, Switzerland
Printing and binding: Kösel, Altusried-Krugzell, Germany
Printed on acid-free paper

**EXHIBITION**
Curator: Mirko Zardini
Design: Bijoy Jain with Mitul Desai; Umberto Riva with Emilio Scarano
Curatorial coordination: Delphine Lesage with Rebecca Taylor
Research: Jayne Kelley, Elliott Sturtevant
Design development: Sébastien Larivière with Catherine Légaré
Graphic design: Common Name, New York

The CCA is an international research centre and museum founded on the conviction that architecture is a public concern. Based on its extensive collection, the CCA is a leading voice in advancing knowledge, promoting public understanding, and widening thought and debate on architecture, its history, theory, and practice, and its role in society today.

The CCA gratefully acknowledges the generous support of the Ministère de la Culture et des Communications, the Canada Council for the Arts, and the Conseil des arts de Montréal.

**Bibliothèque et Archives nationales du Québec and Library and Archives Canada cataloguing in publication**

Zardini, Mirko
Rooms you may have missed: Umberto Riva, Bijoy Jain

(Manifesto)
Catalogue of an exhibition held at the Canadian Centre for Architecture, Montréal, Québec, November 4, 2014 to April 19, 2015.
Issued also in French under title: Des pièces à ne pas manquer.
Co-published by Lars Müller Publishers.

ISBN 978-1-927071-14-4

1. Riva, Umberto, 1928– - Exhibitions. 2. Jain, Bijoy - Exhibitions. 3. Architecture, Domestic - Italy - Exhibitions. 4. Architecture, Domestic - India - Exhibitions. I. Chiaramonte, Giovanni, 1948– . II. Canadian Centre for Architecture. III. Riva, Umberto, 1928– . Works. Selections. IV. Jain, Bijoy. Works. Selections. V. Title. VI. Series : Manifesto (Montréal, Québec).

NA1123.R58A4 2015b     720.92     C2015-941278-1